Out of yOur Hands
But Always in God's...

shELAH

© 2016

Publisher: yOur BackYard
Centerville TN 37033
USA

Revised: 2018

Publications Coordinator: Lahcen Belkimite
Cover Designer: Randall Sandefur
Illustrator: Thushara Sandaruwan Gamage
Marketing Manager: Erin Murphy Anderson
Model for Cover: Autumn Anderson
Editors: Gena Ghant
  B. J. Grainger

Dear Reader,

Remember a time when you knew that things were *Out of yOur Hands*?

I can recount several times in my life when I did not know what to do; when I felt overwhelmed by grief or pain haunted my heart. At times, I wanted to give up. In my desperation, I would cry out to God, "Help me, please…." Each time, although I may not have realized His presence at the time, God touched my life with His loving hand and helped me get through when I could not see any way out.

Out of yOur Hands… shares two of my experiences as well as those of others, who like you and I, have realized that some things this side of Heaven are out of our hands. The stories that others share in this book offer hope and encouragement to look to and trust God; to remember that His loving hands not only control the universe—they reach out in love to help us.

Although not everyone who shares their story in this book professes the same religion and/or believes the same as me, the God of Abraham created each of us. He loves us and tells us that we are to love one another. Because I am a Christian, however, I cannot compromise my belief that God sent His Only Son, Jesus Christ, to die on the cross for our sins; that He lives today; that He is: "The way, the truth, and the life"—the only way to God.

As you read the stories in *Out of yOur Hands*, I pray that you sense the presence of God's hand not only in this work birthed by love—but in your heart. I dedicate this book to you, dear reader.

Sharing yOur stories with love,

shELAH

*Fear not, for I **am** with you;*
*Be not dismayed, for I **am** your God.*
I will strengthen you,
Yes, I will help you,
I will uphold you with
My righteous right hand.

—Isaiah 41:10

With loving thanks...

To my dear friends and co-laborers: Lahcen Belkimite, Erin Murphy Anderson, Bill McDonald, Mary Ellen Bowie, Jill Dudley Cohen, Nathan Wimberly, Deb Walker, Tracy Luttrell, Maria Cline, Tyler Sandefur, B. J. Grainger, and each of you who shared your story with me—thank you.

Thank you for sharing the vision to publish this book of real life stories. I thank God for your encouragement and hard work; for helping bring *Out of yOur Hands* from a dream to a reality. Your love and encouragement reflect the way that God uses the hands and hearts of others to reflect His loving hands.

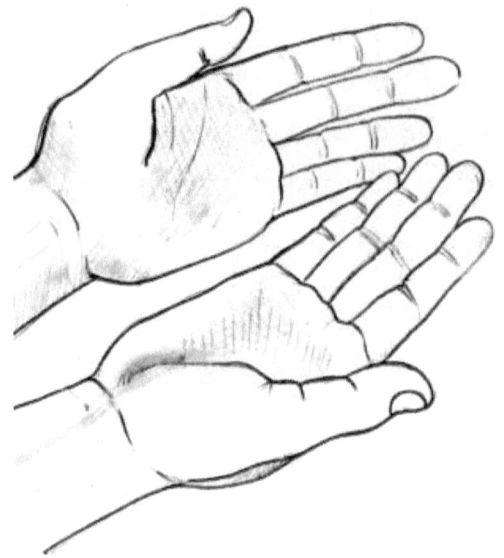

Life-long Choices

Chapter 1: Rising from Drunkenness — 3
Cody McCarver

Chapter 2: Addiction and Trying to Break Free — 9
Tracy Miller-Pickard

Chapter 3: How to Cope Without Drinking — 15
Donna Roberts

Chapter 4: Saved from Drugs and Drinking — 21
Rosemary Fisher

Chapter 5: "Coolness" of Smoking Doesn't Measure Up — 27
Deb Walker

Chapter 6: No More Fear — 33
Joanne Cash Yates

Chapter 7: Choices We Make — 39
Sheriff Bucky

Life-long Lessons

Chapter 8: Whatever You Do—Do Your Best — 45
Lahcen Belkimite

Chapter 9: Make Plans that Will Create Memories — 51
Jill Dudley Cohen

Chapter 10: From Age 16 to 22: A Change of View — 57
Robert Marcus

Chapter 11: How Little We Need to Be Happy — 63
Rosa Alexander

Chapter 12: What the Quest for Happiness Can Lead To — 69
David Baker

Chapter 13: Do Not Quit! — 75
Dave Ramsey

Chapter 14: You Investing in What Counts? — 81
Bill McDonald

Life-long Habits

Chapter 15: From "Fatty" to Healthy and Fit   87
           Tyler Sandefur

Chapter 16: Time to Reduce Salt   93
           Freda Gore

Chapter 17: Whatever You Do, Witnesses Watch   99
           Bob Fu

Chapter 18: How to Care for a Terminally-ill Friend   105
           Deedee

Chapter 19: Prayer: A Source of Aid for Alyssa   111
           Misty Aydelott

Chapter 20: Hugging is Another Way to See   117
           Alyssa Aydelott

Chapter 21: Billy's Story   123
           shELAH

Life-long Memories

Chapter 22: What Daddy Taught Me   131
           Alton Perser

Chapter 23: What You Should Tell Your Parents   137
           Brooke R. Oldenberg

Chapter 24: When Leo Invited Himself Over   143
           Dr. John Hall

Chapter 25: Fighter Turned to Prayer   149
           Jerry "Gator" Arhelger

Chapter 26: I'm Going to Kill Myself"   155
           shELAH

Chapter 27: Never Say Goodbye for Fear You'll Die   161
           Nathan Wimberly

Chapter 28: Struggling to Give God Control   167
           Erin Murphy Anderson

Life-long Choices

*Just as the heavens reign high above the Earth
God's reasons for permitting some things
To happen in our lives,
May surpass our understanding.
Even though we may not understand
Or know the reasons why,
He hears our cries, and when we
Simply trust Him and follow His Will,
He will never fail to see us through.*

Chapter 1

Rising from Drunkenness
by
Cody McCarver

I quit going to church, and seldom thought about God or His will for my life.

At the age of 19, when I realized that I could go into a bar and get paid for singing and playing my guitar, what I had been doing for free in a church—I quit going to church.

Later, after going the way of the world for 25 years, right before I hit bottom and quit drinking for good, I had reached the point where I knew that I would either die from drinking or—I would eventually shoot myself.

During the 25-year span of my life that led up to me knowing that I could not keep living the way I had been, I had acquired just about everything that a guy wanting to be a country artist could desire. Even though I played with a band, owned a tour bus, and was selling CDs in Walmart and other outlets, I realized that my best friend, Jack Daniels™, would ultimately destroy me.

Since I had started drinking regularly at the age of 19, my life had deteriorated to the point I was not only drinking every day,

I experienced frequent blackouts and often did not remember things friends later told me that I did.

Four different times, I drank to the point I developed alcohol poisoning. More times than I care to remember—I could have died, lost without Jesus.

Throughout my last three years existing and fighting to survive as a drunk, from November 2010 to November 17, 2013, I drank a fifth of Jack Daniels™ each day.

Something has to change, I decided, *or I may no longer be here.* At that time, I heard God say, "Cody—that's enough!"

As I started to search for life, joy, and peace in some other way than drinking, I decided to go back to church.

In time, as I sought Him, God squelched my desire to drink with a thirst for His will. He let me know that even though I did not realize it in my past, He had His hand on me the whole time.

As I began to seek God, instead of squandering my life away in a drunken stupor, I realized that He gave me my talents. His will from the beginning was that I would work for Him.

Growing up going to church, I remembered a time when my mother taught Sunday School. I remembered seeing my daddy on his knees at the altar. I remembered learning to play the piano and guitar; learning how to sing. But then, after Mom survived a horrible automobile accident, she became addicted to prescription drugs.

Our family fell apart.

Later, Daddy shot and murdered Mama's boyfriend.

Daddy had served 15 years in a Tennessee prison the last time I visited him in 2013. When I left him that weekend, we both had said, "I love you."

Following that visit, I realized how much I missed the times that Dad and I shared before he went to prison. "God, if You will help me get my dad out of prison," I prayed, "I would sure appreciate it."

On the Wednesday before our next time to visit, Dad and I talked on the phone. "I plan to see you this weekend, Dad," I said.

Instead of my plan—God revealed His.

That Friday, Dad suffered a fatal heart attack. "God, why didn't You answer my prayer?" I cried out in anger.

For the first time ever I experienced what, until that time, I had often wondered about; how God speaks to someone. Without doubt, I knew that God spoke to me that day in the *Still Small Voice* the Bible talks about.

"I did answer your prayer, Cody. I took your dad out of prison. What else do you want?"

When I talked to the prison chaplain about my dad, I learned that Dad had trusted Jesus to forgive him of his sins. Those sins included murder....

The chaplain's words gave me peace that Dad now lives in Heaven.

Today, I also have peace that I will one day live in Heaven with my dad and Jesus. As Luke 22:42 records, because Jesus Christ prayed "Not my will..." and died on the cross for our sins, we can rest assured, that no matter what—God is in control.

At times we get busy, sometimes too busy. When we get too busy to take time to pray... to talk to God... to read the Bible... to go to church... we need to reevaluate the way that we take time. We need to realize that if we don't have the right relationship with Jesus, if our wills do not align with the Lord's will—neither our wills nor we will be right.

When I did not align my will with the Lord's for 25 years and did not go to church; when I wouldn't go, I ended up at my bottom. Now, since I have found out that Jesus is *The Rock* at the bottom, nobody's gonna keep me from going to church.

Today, as I, like many others, struggle with things in life, I not only attend church regularly, I encourage others—don't let anybody in church or any religious person keep you from having a relationship with Jesus. If you go to church—don't quit. If you don't go—you need to start.

shELAH's Note:

Christian Music Artist Cody McCarver, also an actor, spent more than 10 years with the multi-platinum band Confederate Railroad. In 2010, he began his solo music career. In addition to acting in several western movies, Cody has written the sound-tracks for several films.

Cody said that before he started going back to church, "Like a lot of people I thought that church people were just a bunch of hypocrites." Since reestablishing his faith in Christ, Cody states, "I will never let let another person interfere with my personal relationship with Jesus. A life without Jesus is not a life."

The following words from Cody's song, "The Lord's Will, encourage me:

        If you want to hear God laugh,
        Tell Him your plans,
        You don't write that script,
        You're in His hands....

"The Lord's Will," also reminds me of James 4:13-15: "...you who say, 'Today or tomorrow we will go to such and such a city, spend a year there, buy and sell, and make a profit'; whereas [since] you do not know what *will happen* tomorrow. ...your life... is even a vapor that appears for a little time and then vanishes away. Instead you *ought* to say, 'If the Lord wills, we shall live and do this or that.'"

Today, Cody not only attends church regularly, he takes the church to others with his life and music.

In his book, *You Are God's Plan A: And There Is No Plan B*, Dwight Robertson stresses that when Jesus and New Testament writers referred to "the church," they did not mean a building. For the first 300 years of the church, church buildings did not exist. Initially, the word "church" described a group of people God called out. Walls encompass and define buildings. They, unlike people, do not have hands or feet, mouths or hearts.

As Robertson stresses, the possibilities for "the church" to bring God's presence and purposes to people wherever they go do not encompass geographic boundaries. Like Cody, I also believe that we are to regularly meet with others in a church building. Each opportunity we are given, however, whether it may be to join with others in a building or to share ourselves as the church to those who need reassurance of God's love, as the Lord wills—we are not to quit.

When we have lost hope,
Instead of making excuses,
We need to ask for help.
We discover that with help,
Burdens become lighter.
We can get through
What we alone could never do.
And then, as we help others
Get through their tough times
We find
It turns out to be worth it.

Chapter 2

Addiction and Trying to Break Free
by
Tracy Miller-Pickard

"It's not a big deal!"

"Here just try a little. You'll love it."

For me, as with most addicts, this "hook" from someone trying to lure a person into using drugs, proved to be a trap. When I tried "just a little" cocaine the first time, I had no idea that this illegal drug would become the love of my life and that I would ultimately do whatever it took to feed the addiction that devoured my mind during my waking moments. By the time I turned 15 and had tried more than a little crack cocaine, I hated the fact that I landed in my first rehab. My journey in addiction, however, began four years earlier when, at the age of 11, I started trying to fit in and was drinking cough syrup each day before school.

After I became clean, I realized that my destructive behavior evolved from living my early years with fear and feeling abandoned; with seeing my alcoholic father use my mother as his punching bag most nights. I, like most women who become alcohol or drug addicts, used crack cocaine to "'numb' or 'turn off the feelings of anxiety and despair' [that I] ...could not bear to feel; ...to 'escape' from difficult realities, [to] 'run' from distressing thoughts and feelings and 'medicate' emotional pain." I not only wanted to hide my pain, I wanted to feel something—anything other than the empty, lonely, terrified way I felt.

By the time I turned 30, I had been convicted of my first crime and sent to prison with a six-year sentence. Later, I understood that serving time in prison saved my life.

I now know with all my being that at the time, in the deepest depths of my addiction, if I had stayed on the streets in my private prison and not gotten locked up, I would be dead.

Following my release from prison for the first time after serving three years of my sentence, I was not yet capable of being honest about my addiction. When I let myself be around people using drugs, I started right back as well.

Within a few weeks, I lost my freedom again. Today, after getting the help I needed to end the struggle with my addiction, I realize that the only thing that keeps me clean is simple: I take one day at a time.

I don't try to fix tomorrow that isn't even here yet.

I also go to 12-Step meetings where I share my story and listen to what newcomers wanting to stay clean and sober have to say. This serves as a constant reminder of where I came from... where I never want to go back to....

As I surround myself with positive people as well as others also in recovery, I meditate and grow spiritually every day.

I do whatever it takes to stay sober.

At times, staying sober seems easy. Sometimes, recovery proves to be extremely hard. During those bouts when I have my bad days and my life is not all about rainbows and butterflies, I remember that my worst day sober is better than my best day high.

The fight to stay sober is so worth it.

To finally have a life outside of prison, free from fear, without the chains of addiction weighing me down—is more than worth the fight of getting through my bad days—one day at a time. Because I am now sober, I have my family back by my side. God has helped restore the relationships that I had lost with my children.

In addition to being thankful for my relationships with my family... a loving supportive husband who stands by my side, my mother... my children, I thank God for my friends who hold me accountable and won't let me fail. Today I love being happy, joyous—and free.

As I put God first in my life and when I step out of the way and allow Him to work in my life, things go the way they were meant to.

I now tell others still in the struggle of addiction, that I had to stop trying to be the controller of my life and turn it all over to God. I had to allow Him to work in my life.

It's not my will—it always will be His that works for my good.

To help their loved one get to where they are open to treatment and help, I encourage the family of the addict: "You have to be strong and set boundaries. You must not enable the addict. Love them but be careful not to love them to death (literally).

- Don't give the addict money.
- Don't allow them to live in the same house while they are using...
- Don't let them borrow your car...
- Don't bail them out of jail.....

Doing these types of things only allows the addicted person to remain sick in his addiction. It allows him to continue using with no consequences. As long as an addicted person continues to use, there is nothing their family members can do to change the addict. The addict must want help and be willing to take certain steps to get better.

For years, as I abused my drug of choice—everything from alcohol to pills to crack, I was not willing to do what I now know an addict has to do to get help and stay sober. Like many struggling addicts today, I tried, but failed to convince myself of the lie that using illegal drugs or abusing alcohol was no big deal.

Today, after I finally quit making excuses for not getting help, I have been "clean" and free from drugs for almost four years. I now live to help other addicts overcome their struggle with addictions.

To me, it's not only a big deal—it can make the difference between prison, a mental institution, death—or what I choose—life.

shELAH's Note:

Tracy's story reflects the answer to life that Jesus came to give. Matthew 6:33 records that Jesus directed us: "But seek first the kingdom of God and His righteousness, and all these things shall be added to you." Like Tracy, I have learned that when I put God first, this proves to be a really big, big, big deal. Her story inspires me to encourage others to: "Try God's way—Jesus. He's the Way, the Truth, and the Life." When we trust Jesus and follow Him, we not only learn to love Him, we learn to love ourselves—and others.

As we grow in love, God helps us to stop making excuses for staying stuck in addiction or any other problem in life. We learn how to ask for help when we need others to help us.

Addiction and Trying to Break Free

In the article, "The Vicious Truth About Drug Addiction and Alcoholism," featured on Focus on the Family's debagged, Bob Waliszewski, Loren Eaton, and Adam Holz encourage those struggling with addiction and alcoholism that they can be free and clean. These authors propose the following acrostic: **C.L.E.A.N**.

- **C:** Call Out for help.
- **L:** Live... Put your God-given talents to use and have fun with them.
- **E:** Educate Yourself.... Learn truth about substances....
- **A:** Anticipate Adversity. Plan how you'll react to it.
- **N:** Never Give Up. No matter how bad your situation might get, you can always turn things around with enough effort and divine aid. So get on your knees and don't give up.

Our choices determine the course of our life. With Jesus Christ, we have no excuse not to choose to be free and clean from mind-altering, life substances. Because drug abuse and alcoholism destroy lives, they are a big deal.

Jesus Christ, however, and the power over any substance that He offers proves to be an even bigger, greater deal.

Every Day,
God gives us the choice
To run away
Or
Face our problems.

Chapter 3

How To Cope Without Drinking
by
Donna R.

I want a drink...

More often than not, I thought this when I drank vodka to try to solve my problems. Several times, I even celebrated the grand opening of a pack of cigarettes with a fifth of vodka. Instead of dealing with any type of challenge or difficulty in life, whether financial or resentments against those who had hurt me, I chose to drink the problem away. I gave into my desire to numb my pain and feelings and drank myself into oblivion without acknowledging my part in the situations.

In time, I learned from "The Doctor's Opinion" in the *Big Book of Alcoholics Anonymous* (AA), that once I take one drink of alcohol, my body has an allergic reaction and my brain tells me I want more. One more is never enough. Never.

This last time after being in detox for seven days and sober again, I remembered how easily I had forgotten that craving or phenomena that had overtaken my every thought the last time I stayed sober for four months. During the past 11 years, the longest I have stayed sober was 11 months. Now I want to... I have to stay sober. Numerous doctors have warned me. "The next time you drink it could be your last... You keep drinking—you are going to die."

This time, sober again, I not only realize that I have to stop drinking—I want to stop drinking. I do not want to keep experiencing what real alcoholics know... that empty feeling of emotional, mental and physical bankruptcy.

Only we know the feeling of not waking up after a good night of peaceful sleep, but of restless passing out because our bodies could no longer keep up with filtering the amount of alcohol we drank. Only we can know what it feels like to shake so violently when we wake up and realize those last few sips of vodka are gone... until we can get to an open liquor store.

I realize that I cannot stay sober without first and foremost—help from God. I also have to do what I know to be right and use the tools I have learned in AA.

To some, these tools seem like simple, normal, everyday things to choose to do instead of drinking. When those of us who want to stay sober use them, however, they work.

When I started drinking in high school to "fit in," I never imagined I would fall to such a low point in my life; having to search for booze just to get up and function each morning. At that time, I thought of drinking as fun; something all kids went through. Several years later I started drinking more often, especially on weekends when my boyfriend and I would go to a lake to fish or hang out at home. We would drink beer to relax.

At this point, I still did not consider alcohol a problem. In my mind, I had my drinking under "control."

When I poured myself a glass of wine at 9:00 am while preparing lunch on Thanksgiving 2009, I knew I had crossed the line from drinking being fun to an addiction. At times in the past, I had rationalized that wine comes from fruit and people eat fruit for breakfast —*why not have a glass of wine for breakfast?*

After I married Tom, I began drinking vodka with him because I did not like the taste of his drink of choice, whiskey. At first, because of the vodka tasting too strong, I mixed it with orange juice and would drink each night to "relax." As my tolerance increased, I started drinking three to four drinks a night. Next, I started drinking vodka straight from the bottle. After going through rehab my first time, I stayed sober for three months—until I took my first drink. The next time I went through treatment–I stayed sober for six months—until I took my first drink. I stayed sober for 11 months after my last 28 days in rehab—until I took my first drink.

Now, as I pray to stay sober this time and not take that first drink, I have to remember to take my "medicine" and use the tools I have learned. This means that instead of running from my problems and getting drunk, I have to face my problems and trust God to help me. My "medicine" and tools include attending 12-Step groups and dealing with my financial challenges. When I do this and forgive those whose actions hurt me; when I ask for help and begin to work through problems in my personal relationships—I stay sober.

Staying sober helps me remember the good news that some people do care and love me even when I fail. I realize that even though I am powerless without God, I can look to Him for strength. I remember that it's OK to ask God and others who care for me for help. At times when I struggle to refrain from drinking, I can also use the following coping skills:

- Help someone else. I remember how good it felt when I gave a $25 Goodwill gift card to Barbara, a friend just out of rehab for treatment for heroin addiction. Barbara had lost everything, including all her clothes, except those she had been wearing.
- Write in my journal. Recounting things that happened during the day and writing down moments when I experience challenges and how I successfully dealt with my problems, helps me to cope. Writing Bible verses and reflecting on them also helps.
- Go for a walk. Being outside, breathing fresh air and soaking up sunshine frees me from worrying.
- Using my phone's camera to capture images of God's beautiful creations reminds me to be thankful.
- Make a gratitude list. Writing down things that I am grateful for—food, clothes, and having a safe place to stay helps me to become more positive.
- Read a book. Reading not only helps stop my mind from racing—it gives me a sober way to mentally escape from worrying.
- Pray or meditate. In the morning, I need to start my day with prayer and meditation. I need to remember that I can start my day over anytime I take time to pray. Every day, I pray, "Dear God, please help me. God keep me sober."
- Organize something. Organizing a room or space helps me stay focused and better structure my day.

- Make a "God Box" or "God Pocket" in a notebook. Writing down my struggles and putting them in my "God Pocket," gives me a sense of freedom from fears and worries. This helps me remind myself to trust God and—don't give up.
- Set goals. After putting God first in my life, I pray to reach my top priority goal—to reestablish positive relationships with my kids. As God answers my prayers, I move those requests to my gratitude list.

I need to remember that whatever I do—I do not need to isolate myself. I never need to be afraid to tell a friend, my sponsor, or more importantly God, what I am thinking.

As I press forward and figure out my purpose in life, I pray to believe that God has me here for a reason. I pray to remember more that because of Jesus Christ, I am a child of God. Even when I try to hide what's going on with me, He knows my struggles and thoughts. He wants to help me. I also pray that the next time I think I want a drink—I remember that…

shELAH's Note:

Donna said that Matthew 7:7 encourages her, "Ask, and it will be given to you; seek, and you will find; knock, and it will be opened to you." Like Donna, I pray to remember and encourage others to do as Jesus said—to keep asking; seeking; knocking; to know God's will in our lives.

As we prayerfully trust God to face problems in life, we find peace and freedom that nothing else can give—not even a drink.

When you feel that you can't survive,
If your dream shattered
Or
One you loved
No longer cares,
Place your hope in God.
He promises to guide you
He not only cares,
He will help you through
The toughest of times.

Chapter 4

Saved from Drugs and Drinking
by
Rosemary Fisher

I hope no one recognizes me or tries to speak to me, I thought.

At the age of 30, as I sat on the back row of a 12-Step meeting, I had no hope in my life. I felt beyond repair.

I knew I had to find someone or something to help ease the overwhelming pain in my heart soon. If I did not find some semblance of hope, I knew that I could not go on. I felt sure my next step in life would be the one that my mother had taken 14 years earlier when she committed suicide.

Even though I do not remember the name of the woman who spoke at the meeting that night, the story she shared touched my heart. As she talked, the woman's eyes sparkled with hope. I felt an instant bond with her as she said, "I did not have a relationship with my father. I turned to alcohol to try to ease the pain and fill the void I felt inside. I made many mistakes."

The woman speaking not only shared her dark places; she shared words that had helped her move into God's light. Her primary point: "Get off your cross," struck me straight in my heart.

Instead of continuing to hang on her cross, the speaker said, she turned to God. God liberated and freed her.

Some people are afraid to admit they need a Savior; that they need the One Who died for them on the cross, the speaker said. She admitted how desperately she needed God to save her. Transparent and real, she shared her story to give God credit for taking the mess she had made of her life and transitioning it into a beautiful masterpiece. When he opened her door of shame and surrendered it all to Almighty God, she found freedom.

Unlike the speaker, my friends and I were not transparent. Even as children, none of my friends talked about our feelings or things happening at home. At that time, it was easier to simply pretend everything was okay. Like the adage proclaims, I believed: "What happens at home, stays at home."

Each day when I was a little girl, my father, full of rage while under the influence of alcohol, verbally and physically abused me, my brother and our mother. No matter how hard my mother tried to keep my dad calm, nothing she did ever seemed good enough for him.

Dad controlled Mother as completely as one human could control another. He would not even allow her to drive nor did he permit her to have friends. Because I hated how my father treated and controlled our family, I vowed never to let any man control me.

My father's abuse abruptly stopped when he died in a car accident on his 28th birthday. For a brief time at the age of 8, I felt a small sense of relief. Not long after my father's death, however, my mother went wild. She began a lifestyle of drinking alcohol and having relationships with various men. After I turned 14, Mother wanted to be my friend. She would invite me to the bars to drink with her so she would not be alone.

Suddenly, school, sports, and good grades were no longer important to her—or to me. Shortly before my 16th birthday, Mother committed suicide. Without realizing it, I began to build a wall around my shattered heart. Like my mother, I chose a life of drinking, drugs, and promiscuity. At that time, I did not know any other way to kill the pain I hid inside.

That night at the meeting, even at 30-years-old, inside I felt like a scared and hurting little 14-year-old-girl. The woman's story helped me realize that as I had been hanging on my cross, I had never dealt with the abuse my father had inflicted upon me or worked through my mother's suicide.

I realized that I had never confronted those or so many other problems I faced as a little girl. Instead, I learned how to wear a mask and pretend to be someone else so others would like and approve of me.

That night, as the woman spoke, I found hope. Until she shared her story, I had not thought I could have a life worth living. Until that night, I did not know that a person could be a real mess, yet God could use His Hand to transform him or her into a master piece. The love this woman had for Jesus Christ and her willingness to share her story encouraged me to begin my pursuit for her Jesus.

Growing up, when attending church as a little girl, I had heard of God and Jesus Christ. I had religion, I later realized, but not a relationship with Christ.

The woman who spoke at the meeting that night not only had a relationship with Christ, she was madly in love with Him. The power of her testimony began my quest to find Jesus for myself. Her story led to a sacrificial surrender of the life I lived, to a life Christ gave me by dying on the cross for my sins, mistakes, and foolishness.

After that life-changing meeting 15 years ago, I made a commitment to have a relationship with my Savior, Jesus Christ. As I seek Him out by reading Scripture; praying; hanging out with the Holy Spirit, I look forward to every day that I can share my story.

When I share my story, I pray that it will, just as the story of the woman at the meeting did for me, encourage and give hope to others. I pray that those who feel hopeless, like I once felt, will find the only One who can save, deliver, restore and renew them—Jesus Christ.

Until the day I meet Christ face-to-face, I feel honored and privileged to serve Him by serving other women. Today, I am happy when someone recognizes me at a 12-Step meeting. I also thank God for turning my life from a major, massive mess into a blessed, beautiful masterpiece. Now, even though I once felt beyond repair, because of Christ, I know I have hope in my life.

shELAH's Note:

I'm not one of them, I thought.

Years ago when I attended a Narcotics Anonymous (NA) meeting as required for an Alcohol and Drug counselor's class, like Rosemary in her past, I hoped no one I knew would see me.

I don't drink or do drugs, I thought. *Why in the world would I need to associate with those kinds of people?*

During the meeting, as several people shared their stories, it surprised me at just how much I had in common with most of them. They, like me, had experienced struggles with family members. At times, they, just as I in my past, had questioned, *Does God even care about what I am going through?*

Some attending the meeting, like Rosemary and me, had made

peace with God through Jesus Christ. Some appeared to still be seeking the peace that Philippians 4:7 relates: "...the peace of God, which passeth all understanding," that heavenly peace that "shall keep your hearts and minds through Christ Jesus."

You are no different than me, I thought, as several hugged me goodbye as we went our separate ways. But then, I had to reconsider. Yes, I was different from most of them that night. I had hastily prejudged them before I even knew them. They had accepted me unconditionally.

That night, as I bowed my head and asked God to forgive me for so hastily considering "them" as different, I thanked Him. I began to understand why I needed to be at that meeting that night; what God wanted me to see.

I was and still am—one of them.

Rosemary recently completed her 3rd book, The Smokin' Hot Bride of Christ, Exchanging Regrets for Rewards... More about Rosemary: www.rosemaryfisher.com

If you have never started smoking—
Do not start.
If you smoke,
Quit and stay quit.
When you do,
You will not only breathe better,
You will no longer smell like smoke.
In time,
When you quit,
You will become healthier.

Chapter 5

"Coolness" of Smoking Doesn't Measure Up
by
Deb Walker

"Don't ever start…"

I encourage anyone thinking about smoking–"Don't ever start."

I started smoking at the age of 14 after I noticed that other people, particularly my friends, seemed to enjoy doing it. The way manufacturers packaged the cigarettes made them look inviting. *I'm gonna try one of those,* I thought.

I wanted to be cool like the Marlboro™ man who advertised cigarettes on TV.

When I heard warnings from people who either did not smoke or who had quit, particularly someone who had quit because of cancer, I thought: *That will never happen to me,* or *I'll deal with whatever happens, if it comes.*

Sometimes as a teen, I almost felt invisible and at the time I started smoking, I felt nerdy looking. I had straight, *witchy* hair and had to wear cat-eyed glasses. Even though I wore the pink ones with rhinestones on the front of the frame, I still felt like I did not belong. To be accepted, I ditched my glasses; started smoking and drinking.

To me, my friends who smoked looked cool. I wanted to look like and be one of the "in crowd".

One day, I asked Susan, a girl I hung out with, Let me try one of those...." Instead of feeling cool when I smoked my first Marlboro™, I coughed and coughed and coughed.

One of my friends noticed me coughing and said, "These menthol cigarettes are not as dry," and handed me one. I liked the taste of menthol and since it did not make me cough, I started smoking menthol cigarettes.

At first, I only smoked a pack a week.

When I first started drinking, I would wait until Dad fell asleep in his recliner, watching TV while drinking Blatz Beer. Just like clockwork each day after work, Dad would get his beer from the fridge, plop down in his recliner, and turn the TV on. Within 15 minutes and after only a few swigs of beer, he would fall sound asleep. At that time, I would crouch down, sneak over to Dad, grab his beer, chug down a couple of swallows, and run off.

Even though I hated the taste of beer and thought it had to be the most horrid thing I ever put in my small, frail body, I loved the effects. The alcohol took me from reality to the "Land of Oz."

When my dad drank, his mood abruptly changed from Scrooge to Santa Claus. I saw alcohol as a magic formula that cured anything from anger to stress; from boredom to being happy with no cares. Drinking made me feel "10 feet tall and bullet-proof."

As I continued to smoke and drink, these destructive habits increased more and more and more. I could not do one without thinking about the other. For me, smoking and drinking went hand in hand. I don't remember exactly when it happened, but in time, I smoked two packs of cigarettes a day and got drunk on weekends.

"Coolness" of Smoking Doesn't Measure Up

During the 38 years I smoked, I sometimes thought about quitting, but did not have the strength to do so. I did not quit smoking until I gave my life to Christ at the age of 52.

At that time, God not only took away my addiction to cigarettes, He also freed me from my alcohol addiction.

I constantly meditated on the reminder in Philippians 4:13, "I can do all things through Him [Christ] who strengthens me."

Many people have inexcusable excuses as to why they cannot quit smoking. These include: "I'm under too much stress right now." "If I quit, I'll gain weight from eating instead of smoking." "I have to be doing something with my hands."

Several whoppers I have heard cause me to shake my head; things like: "When I'm having an asthma attack, smoking seems to somewhat help relieve it." This one, however, has to top the list of indefensible excuses for smoking: "Smoking helps regulate my bowel movements."

Today, we know so much more of the inherent dangers of smoking than we did back when tobacco companies advertised cigarettes on TV. Contrary to what I thought in my past—smoking is not cool. Nor is it sexy or whatever you may try to fabricate in your brain as a positive reason to engage in this despicable, nasty habit.

Even though wrapped up in a neat little package, smoking contributes to a sure death. It also yellows your teeth, stains your hands, and makes your breath smell like you licked a dirty ashtray.

Hopefully, the reasons I share for not smoking will help persuade someone to not only think about quitting, but—to please quit now. Today, instead of encouraging others to smoke, I encourage smokers: Picture your lungs. In time, if you keep smoking, your lungs will look like a burnt roast instead of a healthy pink, living organ.

As a person continues to smoke, they are experiencing a slow death by suffocation. To someone who thinks or claims that they cannot quit smoking, I encourage them to meditate on Philippians 4:13 or some other positive verse or saying, particularly when they get that urge for a cigarette.

Five years after I stopped smoking, I started experiencing hoarseness. Medical tests revealed that years of smoking had damaged my esophagus. I learned that health problems from smoking may not show up until years after a person quits.

I now encourage others who smoke: Stop now. There's nothing positive about smoking. It does not reduce stress or produce any good thing for or in you. There's no excuse good enough to smoke.

For those thinking about starting to smoke:

Don't ever start....

shELAH's Note:

William Thourlby, a former actor and model, the original Marlboro™ man, admitted that he never smoked. At the age of 89, Thourlby said that his rugged looks in his younger years helped the Marlboro™ cigarette company rebrand itself as a macho smoke.

Even though tobacco companies no longer advertise cigarettes on TV, tobacco use remains the single, largest preventable cause of death and disease in the United States.

Smoking kills more than 480,000 Americans each year, with more than 41,000 of these deaths from exposure to secondhand smoke.

In addition, smoking-related illnesses in the United States cost more than $289 billion a year. This includes at least $133 billion in direct medical care for adults and $156 billion in lost productivity.

Before she quit smoking, Deb, like other smokers, perceived the actors in TV ads for cigarettes, particularly the Marlboro™ man, as cool. Sometimes, in a similar sense, we may only see the pleasure that something offers for the moment and not recognize the ultimate harm it could cause us. We may give in to the seductive pull of that smiling face or curvaceous body.

At times, we may yield to the promise of a thrill, of satisfaction, or release. Too often, we want things that we want right now without considering the consequences. Satisfying some cravings will sometimes kill us. Contrary to what we may think, with God's help, we can actually "live" without the things that we think that we have to have; things that can only temporarily satisfy.

For those who smoke, God can help you "unhook" from cigarettes. I encourage you to remember what Deb said about Philippians 4:13 or whatever "Word" that God brings to your mind. With His help–you can quit.

For anyone who may be thinking about beginning to smoke, I agree with Deb's recommendation: "Don't ever start."

God loves you.
He designed and created you.
He blesses you....
He heals and defends you
Even when you sin
He forgives you
Because
He loves you.

Chapter 6

No More Fear
by
Joanne Cash Yates

God does not love me.

For a long time, I lived a life filled with fear. I thought: *God does not love me.* I also believed what some people seemed to think about me: *Joanne, you are too bad for the Lord to love you.*

Now, I know the opposite to be true. Now, I know my Bible.

For several years following my divorce at the age of 20, I went wild and began drinking and abusing drugs. I considered myself too bad for God to help me. Despite growing up in a Christian home, I did not know the Bible.

The turning point in my life began the Saturday that I and several others, including Johnny Cash, my older brother, encountered a severe hail storm while on a plane. Thankful to have survived the near crash, I attended church the next day.

That Sunday, it seemed that Jimmy Snow, the pastor of Evangel Temple, preached his sermon, "Samson and a Handful of Honey," specifically for me. When Pastor Jimmy invited those who wanted eternal life; who wanted to trust Jesus to save them to come forward, I began to cry and screamed out, "Jesus, save me."

"Jesus loves you, Joanne," Pastor Jimmy reassured me. "He will save you."

After trusting Jesus to save me, I began to study my Bible. The more I read my Bible, the more I realized the vast extent of God's great love for me and how much He loves others. God loved us so much that He gave His Son, Jesus Christ, to die for our sins. God loved me even when I lost hope; when I did not recognize His love. Being married to my husband, Harry, a minister who studied, taught God's Word, and encouraged me, also helped me understand more about God's unconditional love.

From 1975 to 1990, after Harry and I married, we primarily "lived" in a Silver Eagle bus as we traveled to tell others that Jesus loves them. One morning about 2:30 a.m., while we were in bed, Harry said something that abruptly changed the direction we had been heading. God spoke to his heart, Harry said, and told him: "I want you to cancel all your meetings and take your wife and go back home to Nashville."

"Are you sure?" I asked Harry.

"I am sure," Harry said. "The Lord will show you."

Neither Harry nor I was sure at that time how we would be able to do what we were called to do. We had no regular income.

We prayed: "Lord, what are we going to do?"

Later, Harry said that the Lord showed him what we were to do next. What Harry said, however, did not make a bit of sense to me: "Joanne, we are going to start a church in a bar. The bar at the Holiday Inn on Elm Hill Pike is not open for business on Sunday. The Lord has spoken to my heart and reassured me that we can hold church services there."

"You go ahead," I protested. "Not me. God delivered me from the bar scene."

As Harry and I talked and prayed more, I gave Harry an impossible ultimatum. "If...," I proposed. "If the manager of the bar says we can come on in and hold church services and 'if' he does not charge us anything–I will agree."

"If..."

Harry explained his idea of holding church services at the Holiday Inn bar to the manager; stipulating that we could not afford to pay anything.

"It's a hoot—let's do it," the manager said.

Some people, like me when I first heard Harry talk about his dream, challenged him. "What are you doing?" some asked. Others protested. "You cannot hold church in a bar."

During November 1990, the Associated Press ran a story reporting —Johnny Cash's sister and her husband are holding church services in a bar.

The church held in the bar later moved to the Texas Troubadour Theatre and became known as the Nashville Cowboy Church. Now, as then, people hear and respond to the truth that God loves them; that Jesus wants them to trust Him for forgiveness of their sins and gain eternal life. In response to the truth God called us to present, thousands of individuals attending Nashville Cowboy Church have trusted Christ to save them.

During 2015, Nashville Cowboy Church celebrated its 25th "Birthday."

Despite challenges throughout the years, Harry and I, with many others who work with Nashville Cowboy Church, keep on keeping on sharing the gospel.

Today I no longer live a life filled with fear. I know and trust

God's reassurance; revealed in Isaiah 41:10 : "Fear not, for I *am* with you; Be not dismayed, for I *am* your God. I will strengthen you, Yes, I will help you, I will uphold you with My righteous right hand."

Today, I do not worry about what may happen tomorrow. I have read the end of "The Book" and know that God ultimately wins over evil.

I no longer think or believe the lie from the evil one: *God does not love me.* Instead, I trust and believe what God says in His Word. I encourage others that God loves them, even those who, like me in my past, may think they are too bad for Him to love them.

Now, I not only know my Bible, I know without a doubt—*God loves me.*

shELAH's Note:

God's out to get me...

For years, I struggled with the fear that if I did this or that or did not do this or that—God would send me to hell. Due to erroneous "religious" training in my childhood, I considered God to be a condemning, unloving, distant entity out to get me because I repeatedly did what I knew not to do.

Like Joanne, I did not know the Bible or the truths it shares.

Today, I'm thankful that I found a church home where I learned the "Good News," recorded in John 3:16-17 that God was not out to get me or zap me into Hell—but to "save" me. I learned that God loved me and others so much that He sent His Son, Jesus Christ, to die on the cross to pay the penalty for our sins; to give us eternal life.

I learned that the Bible teaches that God does not "send" those who "do" bad things to Hell. Those who reject Jesus Christ as "The

Way, The Truth, and The Life" choose to be eternally separated from Him.

When we trust Jesus Christ and begin to "know" the Bible, we understand that Jesus desires to be a vital part of our lives and guide us with His Spirit. We understand that God not only loves me—He loves you.

You have a story.
So do I.
What we choose to do
Writes our life stories.
I am my choices
You are yours.

Chapter 7

Choices We Make
by
Sheriff Bucky Lee Rowland

In 1977, when only three-years-old, I lost my family in the fire that a teen started in the Maury County Jail in Tennessee. The teen, a runaway, incarcerated in the same facility as my dad, almost died.

After starting a fire in his cell that killed six of my family members, that young man lived. His decision to attempt to kill himself cost other individuals their lives. More than 40 others died from the actual fire or from toxic smoke inhalation.

On that fatal day, my dad, as well as five other family members died during the jail's scheduled visitation. I not only lost my dad, I lost my mother, my grandmother, and three uncles.

Growing up, even though my aunt who raised me did not regularly attend church with me, she encouraged me to go. A neighbor, Elton, a hard-working, strong, Christian family man who lived his faith, took me to church with him and his family.

Even when Elton did not know I was watching him, the way he lived his life aligned with "the Word." He lived the way the Bible teaches us to live. From spending time with and watching

Elton, I learned one of life's valuable lessons. *You never know when someone might be watching you.*

Although I did not often do so, at times, for brief moments when a boy, I questioned God, "Why did my mother die? Why did I have to grow up without a dad?" From living my story, however, I realize what I can now share with inmates as well as those living in the free world: "God has a plan for your life. With Him, you can get through anything."

I stress to those incarcerated where I am Sheriff, "This is not Disneyland. You are where you now are because of your choices. I challenge them to consider this critical life lesson I learned—"You are your choices just like I am mine.

"In the jail and prison settings, because of your choices—you have to deal with the criminal element. You also have to deal with the violent element of society.

"There's a chance you may not be assaulted while you are incarcerated. There's also a chance, however, that you may be. Whatever happens, in and outside of jail," I encourage the inmates, "You don't have to live in fear, but you do need to be aware of your surroundings."

Often, individuals completing their sentences or being bonded out of jail will tell me, "You're not gonna see me back in here again."

"For that to happen you have to start making different choices in life," I remind them. "To stay out of jail—don't put yourself in that same position that got you locked up."

The majority of individuals who end up in jail struggle with a substance abuse problem. Many, who may or may not do something illegal to support their habit, are arrested for not paying child support. Some are incarcerated for theft.

Although it is typically only a few, some in jail appear to be "rotten to the core."

When a young person comes to jail, their parents often have a hard time believing that their child would ever do whatever they did to be arrested. Too often, those with a substance abuse problem will throw their morals to the wind. When actively in addiction, they will beg, borrow, and steal as well as do whatever they think they have to do to support their habit.

I encourage parents who may be in denial and think their son or daughter could not do anything bad enough to end up in jail: "Love 'em... Be there for them, but—don't enable them. If you do, you become part of the problem."

The jail setting gives those addicted to substances the opportunity to dry out and become clean and sober. Currently, here in the Maury County jail, those seeking help can attend AA and NA meetings. We also sponsor job readiness programs and offer parenting and GED classes to help them become better prepared to make it outside the jail setting.

The number one thing a person's needs to enable them to make the right choices in life, I have learned, is to get their heart right with God. This applies not only for those in jail but for each of us. When we choose to trust Jesus Christ, He helps us begin a different way of thinking.

Everyone messes up at times. As corny as it may sound to some, I believe it's amazing what good can come when we choose to go God's way.

I have a story. You have a story.

As we live out our individual life stories, just like I am my choices—you are yours.

shELAH's Note:

When I asked Sheriff Bucky, Maury County Sheriff, "Why are you the sheriff?" he smiled and simply said, "Because of God's plan for my life. Being Sheriff is my calling. You need to know my story to understand."

Knowing Sheriff Bucky's story encourages me to remember that the choices I make determine the path my life will take. A plaque hanging on the wall in Sheriff Bucky's office, which refers to Micah 6:8 reminds those who read it of the choices God wants us to make:

> He has shown you, O man, what is good;
> And what does the LORD require of you
> But to do justly,
> To love mercy,
> And
> To walk humbly with your God?

I believe that the following words, staggered on the plaque, recap Sheriff Bucky's stance regarding choices. When we choose to seek:

> Justice;
> Love;
> Mercy;
> [and]
> To walk humbly with God...

When we trust His loving guidance, then the choices we make ultimately lead us the right way. I pray that I remember to do this more each day.

Life-long Lessons

*Doing the right thing
Means more than
Just saying the words.
Even when you think
No one is watching you,
Do the right thing.*

Chapter 8

Whatever You do—Do Your Best
by
Lahcen Belkimite

"Do you understand me?"

"Do you understand what I mean?"

"Do you speak English?"

"No...," I sometimes had to answer during that fall of 2006 when I first came to America. At that time, I not only struggled to understand what some people said to me, but also how to answer them the right way in my broken English.

As I studied and struggled to learn to speak better English, if I did not understand what someone said to me, I would hand my small notebook and pen to them and ask: "Will you write that down for me, please?"

Even though I was not born in America, I am proud to be an American, I often thought, especially when someone noticed my foreign accent and appeared aggravated that I had not been born here. When someone speaking to me asked, "Are you an American?" I proudly replied, "Yes."

I would smile and say, "Yes, I am an American, and I am also proud to be a citizen."

When someone asked me, "Why did you come here?" I would

answer, "For a better life in a country with more opportunities."

Growing up in Morocco, I often saw myself moving to the United States to live "the American dream."

I may not yet understand some things about my new country, but I am learning more every day.

As I learn, I am not only trying to do things right; I try to do the right things.

In the beginning of my continuing quest to achieve the American dream, doing the right things, working hard and keeping a strong faith in God, helped me reach goals I set for myself.

The first goal I set in America was to work at Home Depot. When I applied for a job there, however, and asked, "Where is the store manager?" several associates either told me: "He's not here," or "He's busy right now."

Instead of waiting at home for someone to call me, I kept thinking about two stances that Martin Luther King Jr. promoted:

- If you want something—Go get it. Period.
- If you can't fly then run, if you can't run then walk, if you can't walk then crawl, but whatever you do—you have to keep moving forward.

As I did not want the government to support me, I made the effort to move forward and "go get" the job at Home Depot. Period. I let the store manager know that I would work hard and do the right things.

Even though the store manager realized that I did not fully understand many things about working at Home Depot, he also saw that I was willing to start at the bottom and do whatever work needed to be done. Within a few months of doing the right things, I went from working part-time to full-time, and receiving a substantial raise.

Doing the right things in my new position as a lot associate (loading products into vehicles) included helping customers to find out their needs. Within less than five years of working at Home Depot, I continued to move forward and received the "Diamond Homer Award" (earned 60 Homer [performance] Awards to attain this status) for basically doing the right things.

Looking forward to reaching another goal, which I had determined that with God's help I would meet, I began working as a Skycap at BWI Airport. In this job, I got to do what I wish more people from all countries would do—help others. At times, I not only helped people carry their luggage, I translated for some travelers whose native languages may have been Arabic, French, or Spanish. I got to help travelers who, like me, were learning English but may have still been struggling with the language.

Each time I received the opportunity, I shared an encouraging smile to let someone coming to America for the first time know that someone understood.

While working at BWI, I met a new friend, a writer and publisher who asked me to share my story in Checkpoints, a news-paper column she writes.

Initially, I laughed and told her, "I'm not a celebrity or a famous person."

Why would anyone want to interview me? I wondered.

shELAH convinced me that everyone has a story to share.

Because I believe that writing can encourage and inspire others, I decided to start working with her company, yOur BackYard Media, as Publications Coordinator.

In my new position, I began to see that writing and publishing books require more work than I imagined. Learning new skills and using my mind to improve myself has been one of my lifetime career goals.

As I have worked to reach my goals, I have surrounded myself with positive people who make a point to try to understand, encourage, and inspire me. Instead of criticizing the way I pronounced some words, they brought out the best in me with words like:

"You're doing good."

"Keep trying...."

"Yes, you can...."

This helped me feel more confident in my ability to improve my English. Encouraging words helped me learn what I now tell others: "If you want to reach your goals, focus on the steps you need to take and don't ever give up, even when someone may discourage you.

"I learned that to reach my goals, I had to listen and learn how to do things the right way. I also learned that if you do not understand something, do not be ashamed to ask for help.

"If you do not struggle with English and have a problem understanding what someone is saying, never criticize or make fun of them." Others, like me when I first started learning English, need someone to listen to them; to help them learn.

I understand what it's like to need help; to feel frustrated when you do not know what someone talking to you means. Today, I not only speak English; I speak the human language—the language of kindness... the language of love for others as we love ourselves.

That's not only one of the right things to do, that's the only right thing to do—no matter our country. I understand that....

shELAH's Note:

Lahcen's story and his encouragement to "do the right thing" reminds me that a multitude of proverbs encourage us to not only do what's right, but to work hard in whatever we do. Many of us who were born in America cannot fully understand what it must be like for someone from another country to become an American citizen; to learn our English language, to understand things that we take for granted. We can, however, make a point to take the time to listen to others; to encourage them; to do the right thing whenever we can—no matter our country.

Knowing Lahcen as a friend and in his work as Publications Coordinator for yOur BackYard Media has helped me to remember that no matter our country of origin, God made each of us unique. He has given us gifts to share with others.

God not only loves Americans, He loves people from all countries throughout the world. He causes the rain to fall on everyone, not just some people.

Lahcen's story reminds me to not only remember to thank God for things I sometimes take for granted in America, it encourages me to also try to understand, help, and love others more.

Like Lahcen, I believe that when we do things right as well as do the right thing—no matter our country—we can't go wrong.

"Do you understand me?"

As you navigate your way through the world
No matter where you are
My heart remains connected to yours.
The unbreakable bond
Between a mother and her child
Never ends.

Chapter 9

Make Plans that Will Create Memories
by
Jill Dudley Cohen

I'm not ready....

Tomorrow will be exactly 19.5 years since my son, Bradley, entered into my world and made me his mom. Tomorrow, Bradley will be moving into his own apartment. Even though I know he's excited and ready to live on his own–I'm not ready.

During the tomorrows when I will wish Bradley were still at home... During the times, we talk on the phone... At times, when we will get together and make new memories, I will be ready.

I will do as Mother and I do when we share times together, I will often recount the memories we made as a family, the fun times and even those when we may have shed a tear. I will say to Bradley, "Remember the time when...?"

If I knew I only had one hour to talk with Bradley or someone else I love, I would reminisce about fun memories that we had shared.

Although the love our family shares with each other goes without saying, I am sure I would say, "I love you." My family and

I love each other. We say, "I love you" often and end each phone conversation with those three words.

If I knew the time I shared with someone I loved would be our last time together, however, instead of repeatedly reassuring them, "I love you," I would spend my time reminiscing.

I might reminisce about growing up as an only child in a "Don't speak until spoken to environment." At that time, in my prim, proper, protected, and respectful childhood, I did not say much. As I listened, however, I learned. Learning to respect and honor my parents instilled the value of respecting others.

In my last conversation with someone I love, I would likely share some things I learned as a child as well as some life lessons I have learned in my work as a *Registered Tax Return Preparer*. Some of the following things which I practice in preparing taxes for clients also prove helpful in my everyday life.

- Listen. I encourage others to listen intently to those they communicate with. When interviewing a client to gather tax information or talking to someone to find out more about them, I confirm what I hear them saying. I say something like, "What you are saying is..." While chatting with a client, I am simultaneously gathering information for deductions. when talking with a friend or someone I love, I am likewise gleaning information to nurture our relationship.
- Keep it real. Encourage those who own a business to be realistic regarding their expectations. Not everybody in business makes a fortune. "If what you are doing in your business is working—great," I tell a business client. "As long as you have enough money for food and shelter,

Make Plans that Will Create Memories

if you do not owe lots of money, and you are not in financial trouble—wonderful. You do not have to make a lavish amount of money to be a success. "Don't just settle for second best. Do something you enjoy doing. In business and in life, when you have love, family, fun, and respect—you have it made in life."

➢ Ensure mutual trust and respect. I encourage others to remember that whether seeking a tax preparer, building positive familial bonds, or searching for someone to share a strong, nurturing relationship with—"You need someone you can trust and respect—someone who, at the same time, trusts and respects you. You also need to be trustworthy and respectful."

➢ Be ready. Make sure you have everything you need to file your taxes lined up. I encourage my clients to bring all the financial information they have for me to review. To reassure them, I say, "If you are missing something, I will help you get it." In life, we also need what is necessary to accomplish our dreams and goals lined up. When we realize that we are missing something, we need to be willing to ask for help. We also need to help others when they need our help.

When reminiscing in a final conversation with someone I love, I would likely encourage them to listen... to keep it real... to never settle for second best... to ensure mutual trust and respect in their relationships—to be ready.

Be ready?

As Bradley leaves home, I am so proud of and happy for him.

He possesses wonderful life skills and has proven himself to be incredibly competent. As he takes charge of his own home, Bradley will be able to decide whom to welcome inside. He will be able to determine what goals and dreams to pursue in his life. He will be able to use his manners, tact, and life lessons to navigate through the world. I know that Bradley is not only able—he is ready....

At times when I think, *I'm not ready*, I need to "Remember the time when..." exactly 19.5 years ago, God made me a mom when He gave Bradley to me; to our family.

As I thank God for the unbreakable bond between a mother and her child—no matter where that child may be, I also say to Bradley, "Thank you for being my son."

shELAH's Note:

Love, love, love Jill's reminder of the unbreakable bond between a mother and her child. I also love David's reminder from Psalm 139, of the unbreakable bond between our Heavenly Father and His children:

> Where can I go from Your Spirit?
> Or where can I flee from Your presence?
> If I ascend into heaven, You are there;
> If I make my bed in hell, behold, You are there.
> If I take the wings of the morning,
> And dwell in the uttermost parts of the sea,
> Even there Your hand shall lead me,
> And Your right hand shall hold me.
> How precious also are Your thoughts to me,
> O God! How great is the sum of them!
> ... lead me in the way everlasting.

Make Plans that Will Create Memories

David's reassuring words remind me that no matter where we or our children may be—God, as well as His thoughts and love, remains ready to lead us in the everlasting Way, Truth, and Life.

Because we never know how much time we have to share with someone, like Jill, we need to remember to make our moments count. We also need to reassure our loved ones that they remain in our thoughts, prayers and love.

When we and our loved ones go our separate ways, because we have made fun, loving memories, we will not regret something we did not do… something we did not say.

No matter whether we are ready or not…

Sometimes, when growing up,
We do not appreciate
The people God has placed in our lives;
Those who care for and nurture us,
Who provide what we need
Until
They are no longer there.

Chapter 10

From Age 16 to 22: A Change of View
by
Robert Marcus

"What are you doing?"

When I, at the age of 16, yelled those words out to my mom, I had just come home to find her in my room. "I was looking for my keys," Mom said.

When I noticed that Mom, actually my step-mom, had moved some of my belongings around, I narrowed my dark eyes to stress that I did not believe what I considered a lame excuse for her to go through my things.

From that point, my anger escalated to the explosion of a barrage of hurt feelings that I had held inside. "You have no right to invade my privacy!" I yelled. "You would never treat your own children the way you treat me. Just because you don't love me like you love them does not give you the right to come into my room without my permission."

By the time I finished berating Mom that day, she left my room in tears.

Good, I thought, feeling vindicated that my harsh words had made her cry. *Maybe you will think about what you are doing and not cross that line next time.*

I did not learn that lesson until being out on my own for several years. Now, I realize that verbally attacking my mom was not the way to go about addressing my frustrations. What I did was an awful thing to do. At that time, even in the midst of my anger, I wanted Mom to reassure me, in spite of the wall between us and even though I was her step-son, that she loved me.

Later, I remembered that several times before I left home at the age of 18, Mom had made a point to reassure me. She often told me, "I love you, Robert."

After one of those times, I had protested: "But you never take the time to sit down and talk with me."

"I want to, but you seem to have put up a wall between us that I don't know how to get through," Mom tried to explain.

When I left home to move in with Lawrence, my biological brother three years older than me, I still held onto resentment toward Mom.

As my first job in Dallas working for Papa John's Pizza turned out to be awful, exactly what I expected, my resentment toward Mom started to dissipate. With this initial taste of corporate structure and several following jobs, I started to recognize some of my own short-comings and the validity of some of the things Mom had shared with me. I realized that I had constructed a wall between me and others. Too often, I did not know how to open up and share the real me.

Working in sales during the next year helped me begin to develop people skills. I learned to approach people and find common interests with them. Instead of operating only out of my own personal feelings, I learned to interact with others, consider their interests, and present positive information.

While living with Lawrence and then later with others, I learned to appreciate Mom and Dad. At home, I never even considered that somebody had to pay the mortgage, electricity, and water. I did not appreciate that Mom and Dad always made sure we had food in the house. While away from home, learning these real-life lessons sometimes felt like a "smack in the face."

Several times, when I and others did not pay our bill, the electric company cut off our electricity. Twice, we had to move after our landlord threatened to evict us for failing to pay our rent. Some days, we ran out of food and had to ask for help from a local food bank. Once, we did not have water for three months after we could not afford to pay a $1,000 water bill.

My "smack in the face" life lesson taught me that to survive in real life, I had to work regularly, pay my own bills, and manage my money. Ultimately, I managed a kitchen in a restaurant where I earned a decent salary. Here I learned that I could not pursue my goals if I continued to support those I lived with who chose not to work, but to use drugs or alcohol instead.

When Mom called and told me that Dad's health problems had worsened and asked me to consider moving back home, I did not hesitate to say yes. This would simultaneously help them and let me take a step back from the stressful life I had been living. When Mom added, "We miss you," I knew what I had to do.

I had to not only go back home and be there for my family, I had to apologize to Mom.

I knew Mom loved me because she took care of me when I was sick. She took me to the optometrist and had purchased the eye glasses I needed. She made a point to be there for me—even when

I had struck out in anger toward her. When I saw Mom again, I gave her a hug and told her, "Even though I had doubted it at times, being out on my own made me realize just how much you and Dad love me."

After I had taken down the wall I had erected between us, Mom and I could talk. If I could have told myself back then, what I know today at the age of 22, I would have said:

- Don't let your anger cloud your judgment.
- Don't hold onto your anger or bottle up your feelings inside until they explode.
- Don't let your feelings control you, but do what you know to be right.

I would also remind myself back then to do what I try to remember to do today—to ask myself the question before I react in anger to something that upsets me: "What are you doing?" Answering this question and thinking things through instead of blowing up in anger can help keep you from hurting someone you love and care for; someone who cares for and loves you—more than you realize.

shELAH's Note:

At times, those with parents who care for and love them, like Robert at 16, may not realize that their parents deserve respect and honor. Some, like me at one time, may question, "How do you honor a Mom or Dad who does not deserve to be honored?"

Gayle Jackson addresses this challenge of how to honor an abusive parent in her book, *Honoring Your Parents*. She states: "It would be so much easier if God had asked only that we honor our parents if they are good, kind and loving to us, but unfortunately this Commandment says honor your father and mother. Period." The Fifth of the Ten Commandments, Exodus 20:12, specifically stresses: "Honor your father and your mother, that your days may be long upon the land which the Lord your God is giving you." For many hurt, abused, and damaged people, including me in my past, this Commandment proves nearly impossible to obey. Jackson encourages:

> The first thing we have to remember is that God is our loving Heavenly Father who does not just slap down a rule and sit back waiting for us to disobey it. His rules and precepts are there for one reason only—our ultimate good. If we truly desire to obey Him no matter how impossible it seems, He is willing and anxious to help us....
>
> ...He is the only one who can change emotions and attitudes and mend damaged relationships and broke[n] hearts.

Robert's story reminds me to not only remind children to honor their parents but to also encourage parents and children to consider the question: "What are you doing?"

When we as children and parents do as God directs—when we honor, forgive, and love one another—we show those we love and care for; those who care for and love us—the love, care, and honor that they and we deserve.

During trying times
When one may not have an abundance
of food or other things,
We find the answer
In
Love and sharing.

Chapter 11

How Little We Need to Be Happy
by
Rosa Alexander

Even though we had some money, too often the stores had little or no food for us to buy.

Living in Transylvania during the Ceausescu regime, because of the shortages, we regularly had to ration our food to ensure we had something to eat throughout the month. That trying time taught me: *How little one needs to be happy....*

That cold December day in 1984, when I saw Julia, my 9-year-old daughter, sitting at our kitchen table waiting patiently to help me bake a Christmas cake, my heart melted. "First, we have to decide what kind of cake we want to bake," I said.

"I would like to bake two kinds of cakes, Mummy. A chocolate one and a lemon one. How much flour do we need for each cake?"

"Julia, today we can only bake one cake. We do not have enough butter to bake two. What kind of cake do you think would be good for us to bake?"

"How about a chocolate cake?" Julia asked.

After I poured just the right amount of flour into the oversized, white porcelain bowl that Mother had used for mixing cakes and breads when I was a little girl, I gave Julia step-by-step directions. "Now we add a little bit of salt and baking powder, and set this mixture aside while we mix the sugar and butter in the other bowl."

I sighed as I sliced off a little less butter than I would have normally used, creaming it in with the sugar. *One day,* I thought, *when there is no longer a shortage of butter or flour or sugar, we would bake a chocolate and lemon cake at the same time.*

Next, Julia beat the eggs with a fork and poured them in with the butter and sugar mixture. We then blended the cocoa, flour mixture, and milk together. In less than an hour after we had started mixing the cake, Julia and I sat across from each other at the table, laughing, and talking while sharing an oversized slice of chocolate cake.

The food shortages in Romania began subtly a few years earlier, but with the growth of the Ceausescu regime's power, the dearth of food steadily worsened. Each month I knew that if I did not carefully budget our rations of food, we would run out of some of our basic food staples. Shelves in stores that in the past had overflowed with a barrage of products were now empty. No one, however, seemed to have any rational explanation for the food shortages.

We did not have to struggle as hard as some families because both our parents regularly gave us vegetables from their gardens. Some weeks, our parents would bring us a chicken. Because I worked as a manager of the local mall in Kingstown, I had a few special connections and could sometimes even purchase coffee.

Not until I went to check on a neighbor one day, did I realize just how severe the food situation had become. For supper that night, Aniko, in her mid-30s, told me that she, her husband, and their two boys again ate what they had been eating for each meal during the past week: An onion, sliced and marinated in vinegar, and a baked potato.

"Yesterday, I stood in line for eight hours to buy our monthly two-pound ration of meat," Aniko said. "When I finally reached the front of the line, the manager told me, 'Sorry. We have run out of meat.'"

Aniko stormed over to her fridge and yanked open the door. Her finger shook as she pointed inside. "It is empty," she said. "Rosa, I do not know what to do. For two weeks our family has not had any meat. Next week, we will run out of onions and potatoes."

When I went back home I opened my refrigerator, took out the one-pound package of ground pork I had and divided it in half. I wrapped the meat in wax paper and told Julia, "Here. Please take this and give it to Aniko."

Julia never questioned us sharing what little we had with a neighbor who had even less. I had taught her from an early age that we had to love and help each other if we were to survive.

When shortages abounded and our future seemed so uncertain in my beloved Transylvania, I realized: How little one needs to be happy. All we need to do is love one another.

Even though there were more and more shortages and hard times, Alan and I deliberately cherished our times together as a family. We knew how to survive. As we sometimes did not have running water for several days, we collected and stockpiled rainwater for times when the water would be cut off. We also kept the bathtub full—just in case...

When the weather turned too cold for Julia and Peter to sleep in their bedrooms, we huddled together in one room. In the evenings, we talked about what we had done that day. We played games together. At night, after saying our prayers, Alan and I would tell Peter and Julia stories until they fell asleep.

Today, I encourage others to remember—love is the answer to everything. When we begin to share love with others, we have even more love to give because love, I have learned, is infinite. I have also learned that the more we love others without any expectations— the more empowered we become. We no longer have to search for love when we have it in our power to give.

During those trying times years ago, Alan, my husband, our son, Peter, Julia, and I learned one of life's most valuable lessons firsthand. Even when one may not have an abundance of food or other things, there need not ever be—no shortage of love.

shELAH's Note:

In America, because most of us have an abundance of food, we may forget that some people in our own country, as well as as throughout the world, sometimes struggle with having enough to eat. The Bible notes that Jesus notices those who care for those who are hungry. In Matthew 25:37, He tells of a time in the future when He will remind people of how they responded to those who needed food and were hungry while they lived on Earth: "inasmuch as you did *it* to one of the least of these My brethren, you did *it* to Me."

Mother Teresa, a Catholic nun who lived among and cared for the poor in Calcutta for 50 years, shared the following:

> ➢ I used to pray that God would feed the hungry, or do this or that, but now I pray that He will guide me to do whatever I'm supposed to do, what I can do. I used to

pray for answers, but now I'm praying for strength. I used to believe that prayer changes things, but now I know that prayer changes us and we change things.

- Even the rich are hungry for love, for being cared for... for being wanted... for having someone to call their own.

In addition to feeding literal food to the hungry, God shows us those who need to be fed in our backyards. We are to "feed" love to the hearts of others and help nourish them spiritually.

We are to love and reassure others that God loves them.

As Rosa stresses, "Love is the answer to everything."

When we love others as God loves us and share with those in need, we will also realize what Rosa reminds us: *How little one needs to be happy.... All we need to do is love one another.*

God's perfect plan for our life,
Like the Heaven above Earth
Supercedes
Any plan our mind might conceive.
God's will, not ours,
Makes us happy.

Chapter 12

What the Quest for Happiness Can Lead To
by
David Baker

I am going to live my life to make me happy.

As a young man, I wanted to be happy more than anything. I repeatedly told my parents, "Look, it's my life-not yours. You had your chance to live your life to make you happy. Now, I am going to live my life to make *me* happy."

According to friends, I needed to drink, do drugs, party, and fool around with girls to be happy. For a while, I did just that and more. Some of the time, I even had fun.

Drinking, doing drugs, partying, and fooling around with girls, however, failed to make me happy. Inside, I felt empty.

In my heart, I knew something was missing. For the next eight years, I tried the "pleasures of sin" and doing the things "the world" offers to try to make me happy. After making the decision to yield to follow God's way, I realize that those eight years were not only futile, but eight years too long.

Today, in my work as a chaplain for Maury County Jail in Tennessee, I talk to people every week who have spent 10, 20,

30, or even more years, searching for true happiness. Those who continue to search for the happiness the world claims to offer find that their efforts fail. Hebrews 11:25 in the Bible says that one may experience pleasures in sinning, but they only last for a season; for a little while. Then the consequences of sin begin.

The consequences of sin last much longer and far outweigh any pleasure they may offer. For example, how much pleasure does alcohol really bring?

I often ask an inmate, "How much fun can you have from the time you start drinking and get a slight buzz until you don't remember anything?" When they start telling me, "It depends," I say, "I realize it depends on what you drink, how fast you drink, how much you weigh, and what you have had to eat, etc., but a 'good buzz' will only last a few hours.

"How long do the consequences of drinking last?

"How long does the hangover last? How long does the DUI last?

"How long does the divorce last? How long does losing your family last? How long do 'the stupid things we do when drinking' last?

"Each one of those things lasts longer than the fleeting 'pleasures of sin'. How much pleasure do you get in using drugs? I realize this also depends on what drug you use and how much, but the effects usually only last for a few minutes or a few hours.

"How long do the consequences of using drugs last?

"How long is the jail sentence? How many relationships do you and your drug abuse destroy? How long does the probation last? How many drug tests will you now have to take? How much money will you have wasted?"

What the Quest for Happiness Can Lead To

From my own and the personal experiences of those I work with, I know that the consequences of sin always last far longer than the pleasures.

I also know that the consequences of sex with a woman outside marriage last much longer than the pleasures. How about 18 years of child support? How about a lifetime of a disease? Sad that we trade temporary pleasures for eternal ones; for eternal treasures.

When we spend time with God and do His will, we can have pleasures for evermore. Those pleasures do not start just when we get to Heaven; they can start right now.

When I surrendered to God to preach the Word of God, and to do His Will, I thought I would have a miserable and boring life. I was accustomed to the "thrill" of alcohol, drugs, women, parties, fast cars, and jumping out of airplanes.

I not only thought that serving God would not be any fun; I expected to be miserable.

A few weeks after surrendering to God, I woke up one morning thinking about my life and how happy I had become.

Wow, I thought, *I have not taken any drugs, consumed any alcohol, or touched a girl, yet I'm happy.*

At that time, my happiness did not make sense to me.

I decided to do a Bible study on happiness. What I learned amazed me.

I learned:
- We are happy when we are serving (1 Kings 10:8);
- We are happy when God corrects us (Job 5:17);
- We are happy when we make the Lord our God (Psalm 144:15);
- We are happy when we find wisdom (Proverbs 3:13);

- We are happy when we have mercy on the poor (Proverbs 14:21);
- We are happy if we suffer for righteousness (1 Peter 3:14);
- We are happy when we fear God (Proverbs 28:14);
- We are happy when we keep [...God's] law (Proverbs 29:18).

In the past, I had thought that if I obeyed the law (meaning the Bible), I would live a boring, miserable life. I learned the truth that God said that if I would just keep His law, I would be happy. I realized God knew a lot more about life and much more about what would make me happy than I did or ever could.

Today, I encourage others that instead of thinking: *I am going to live my life to make me happy*—Why not give God a chance?

I also challenge those in jail to fully live for God for six months and see if they are not so much happier than they ever could have been in the world.

It works. I not only know that from my own and the personal experiences of others—God's Word says so.

shELAH's Note:

The phrase "happy is" occurs in the KJV of the Bible 11 times. Proverbs 16:20 in the NKJV states, "He who heeds the word wisely will find good, And whoever trusts in the LORD, happy is he." This verse reminds me that when we have faith and peace between ourselves and God, trusting Him and accepting His gift of eternal life that Jesus died on the cross to give us—we will know true happiness. We do not have to do as Chaplain David did in his past —*try to live my life to make me happy.*

What the Quest for Happiness Can Lead To

When he wanted to be happy more than anything and tried fitting in with friends, by having sex outside of marriage, drinking and doing drugs, Chaplin David found his life miserable and empty When he gave his life to Christ, he began to understand that we "are not our own" because of the price Jesus paid to save us. He learned what it means to be happy.

When you and, I like Chaplin David, serve God by following Jesus and sharing His love, we are not only at peace—we are happy.

If the reflection you see
In the mirror
Makes you want to break it,
Don't break the mirror.
Ask God to change the heart
Of the one the mirror reflects.

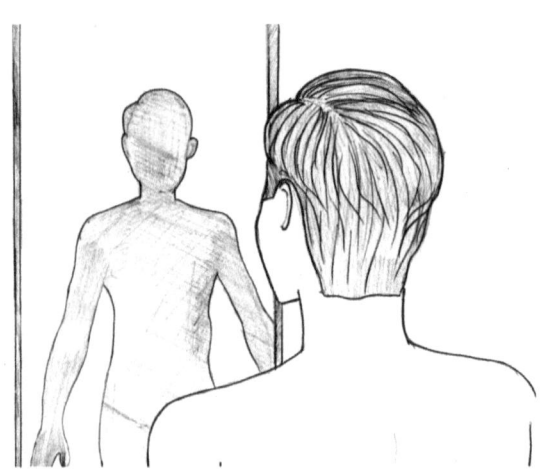

Chapter 13

Do Not Quit!
by
Dave Ramsey

I remember wanting to quit.

At one point in my life, I wanted to lie down somewhere, curl myself into a fetal position and cry out: "I give up. I quit. Don't kick me again."

At that time in my life after I went bankrupt, I felt like a failure in the financial world. Instead of giving up, however, I am thankful that God helped me begin a quest to find out how money really works. I wanted to learn how I could take control of my finances and handle money the right way.

I read everything I could get my hands on relating to money. I interviewed older rich people—people who made money and kept it.

My quest led me to a really, really, really uncomfortable place —my mirror. I came to realize that my money problems, worries, and shortages primarily started and stopped with the man in my mirror. I also realized that if I could learn to manage the character I shaved the face of every morning, I would win with money.

I went back to my first love, real estate, to get out of debt. Along the way, I began another path—to help others, literally millions of individuals take the same quest to the mirror.

With God's help, I did not quit.

Today, I have an unusual way of looking at the world. My wife, Sharon, says I'm weird, and, truthfully, she's right. But there's a reason. Starting from nothing, by the time I was 26 I had a net worth of a little over a million dollars. I was making $250,000 a year. That's more than $20,000 a month net taxable income.

I thought I was having fun—98% of the time.

But 98% truth is a lie. That 2% can cause big problems, especially with $4 million in real estate. I had a lot of debt, a lot of short-term debt.

In time, I had to admit—I'm the idiot who signed up for the trip. Debt caused Sharon and me, over the course of two and a half years of fighting it, to lose everything we owned. At the time, we did not share our struggle with others or tell anyone what was going on.

If we had to do it again, we would learn from the wisdom of others who have been through what we were going through. We soon learned that we were not the only ones at the bottom. Although some considered us to be like Mattel's Barbie and Ken, the couple who appear to be perfect... perfect clothes... perfect car... perfect house—we were broke.

Today, I encourage others: "Don't take financial advice from broke people." I don't.

In 1992, I formed Ramsey Solutions to counsel folks hurting from the results of financial stress. I've paid the "stupid tax" (mistakes with dollar signs on the end) and learned from those mistakes. Hopefully, what I share will help some of you so that you won't have to do the same thing. Based on all that Sharon and I had learned, I wrote the book *Financial Peace* to help others.

After I began selling *Financial Peace* out of my car, I started a local radio call-in show with a friend of mine, *The Money Game*. This nationally syndicated radio show, now known as *The Dave Ramsey Show*, helps others recover from financial disasters like the one I survived. My prayer is that this "show" will help show others how to succeed financially.

Many companies define success based on the dollars coming in. At Ramsey Solutions, we define our success by the number of lives changed: listeners getting out of debt, readers taking their first *Baby Steps* and saving $1,000. We encourage people—Don't give up when you have failed financially. Don't quit.

At some time in their lives, most people feel like quitting. You may feel like quitting when you look at your life situation and it seems that not one thing has turned around for good in a long time. You may feel discouraged because someone cheated you or lied to you.

You may feel like giving up what you know you are called to do because you have not yet found your right place in life. During his speech October 29, 1941, Winston Churchill told the boys of Harrow School:

> Never give in—never, never, never, never, in nothing great or small, large or petty, never give in except to convictions of honour and good sense. Never yield to force; never yield to the apparently overwhelming might of the enemy.
>
> Do not quit.

shELAH's Note:

Dave's recount of a time in his life when he felt like giving up encourages me. Matthew 14:34; 36; 38, recounts a time at a place called Gethsemane, shortly before Jesus was crucified. Here He struggled regarding what He would have to endure to pay the penalty for our sins. He told His disciples: "My soul is exceedingly sorrowful, even to death." Jesus prayed: "Abba, Father, all things are possible for you. Take this cup away from Me; nevertheless, not what I will but what You will."

Jesus did not give up even when He later found his disciples sleeping while He had been praying. He warned as well as encouraged them with words that aptly apply to us today:
"Watch and pray, lest you enter into temptation. The spirit indeed is willing, but the flesh is weak."

If we or someone we know should feel like curling up in a fetal position and crying out: "I give up. I quit"—may we remember to follow Jesus directives: "Watch and pray"—trusting our Heavenly Father to strengthen our flesh.

The following poem encouraged me at a time in my past, when I felt discouraged:

> When things go wrong as they sometimes will,
> When the road you're trudging seems all uphill
> When the funds are low and the debts are high,
> And you want to smile, but you have to sigh,
> When care is pressing you down a bit --
> Rest if you must, but don't quit.
> ~ Author Unknown

The words from the anonymous writer of that poem, as well as those from Winston Churchill and Dave, remind me of the power of words.

Words, as the Bible reminds us, have the power of both life

and death. At times, when we get discouraged or see someone else falter; struggling to "keep on keeping on," we can remind them that God can get them through. Despite and in the midst of troubled times, we can pray and encourage ourselves and others with words that have encouraged us to:

"Never give in—never, never, never, never quit."

We can also, as Dave encourages others, "learn from the wisdom of others who have been through what we were going through." With God's helping hands using the abilities He gives us, we can not only refuse to quit, we can appreciate the reflection of the one we see in the mirror.

*Instead of counting the hours in our days
Longing to do the things we enjoy,
We would do better
To treasure
The moments...
To make our days count
Enjoying the things we do.*

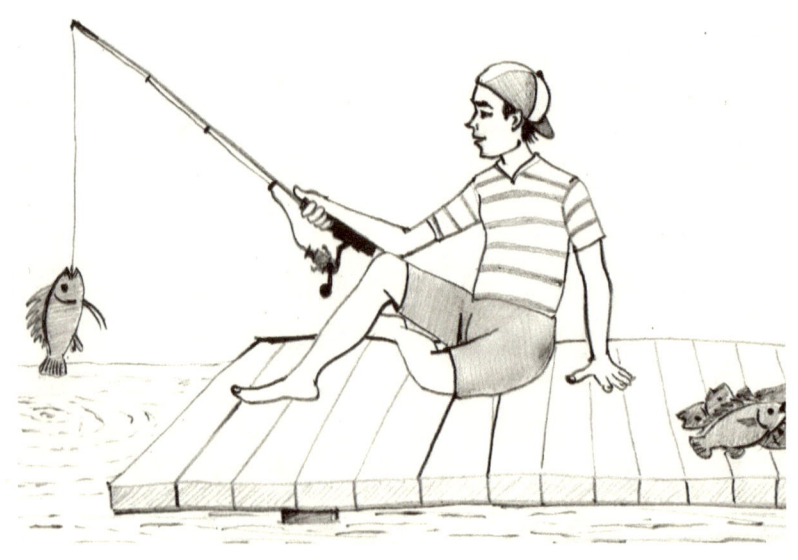

Chapter 14

Are You Investing in What Counts?
by
Bill McDonald

"Dad, I gotta talk to you."

That day, years ago, I could not wait to tell Dad about my day. At the age of 13, I knew I had just experienced one of the greatest days in my life. At that particular time, however, Dad was busy talking to several other people.

"Bill, you go and wait for me in my office," Dad said. "I will be there in a few minutes."

While waiting for Dad, I grinned; remembering the fun I had fishing earlier that day at Beaver Dam. Within the first hour, I had caught seven trout. By the end of that day, I caught a total of 42 fish. As the limit of the number of fish a person could keep was only seven, I released 35 of the trout.

"What do you need to tell me, Son?" Dad asked when he walked into his office.

"Dad, I just caught 42 trout today," I blurted out.

"You have done well," Dad said with a smile. He hesitated for a moment as he locked his eyes into mine. "Was what you did today worth what it cost you?"

"Definitely," I said. "It cost me 10¢ for hooks. I only spent another 10¢ for a sinker... 24¢ for a can of whole kernel corn."

"No—you actually spent more than that."

"Oh yes," I said. "It cost Mom gas to drive me there."

"No," Dad said, "what you did today cost you one day of your life to get to do it. Was what you 'spent' today worth that?"

Then and now, I have to say, "Yes...."

John 10:10 records what Jesus shared about His reason for His time on earth: "I have come that they may have life, and that they may have it more abundantly." That day in his office, Dad stressed that each day I needed to remember not to merely talk about what I wanted to do in my life, I needed to make a point to "do life"; to live the abundant life that Jesus came to secure for us.

Psalm 90:12, often associated with the thought of death, states: "So teach us to number our days, That we may gain a heart of wisdom." That reminder, nevertheless, is not about death. It is totally about living life; about living real life every day—about living life now.

Looking back on that day years ago, when I could not wait to tell Dad my fishing tale, I still consider my day fishing well worth the investment. I not only experienced the thrill of catching 42 trout, I got to spend a day in nature. I had time to be alone. I lived moments I still treasure.

shELAH's Note:

William Wallace (1270–1305), who fought for Scotland to be freed from England's king, was once condemned as a traitor. In time, he became known by the Scots "as a martyr and as a symbol of the struggle for independence, and his efforts continued after his death." For his fight, Wallace "was hanged, disemboweled, beheaded, and quartered." While he lived, Wallace stressed: "Every man dies. Not every man really lives."

Grandma Moses, who painted her first picture when she was 76 years old, began working for a farmer neighbor at the age of 12. She married at age 27 and raised a family of five children. Along with sewing and other domestic tasks, she cooked vegetables raised in her family's garden.

When Grandma Moses' "arthritic hands forced her to abandon embroidery; she took up oil painting in the 1930's. For a while, she sold paintings (and pickles) at the county fair, while also having a group of works on display in the local drugstore's window."

Before she died at the age of 101, Grandma Moses said: "I look back on my life like a good day's work; it was done and I am satisfied with it." 2 Timothy 4:7 records that Paul, like Grandma Moses, felt good about his days at the end of his life: "I have fought the good fight, I have finished the race, I have kept the faith."

Each day, we would do good to do as Bill, William Wallace, Grandma Moses, and Paul did: remember to consider the costs of what we do each day. That way, when we say "Goodbye" to our time on this earth, we can look back knowing that we have really lived.

*God grant me the serenity
to accept the things I cannot change,
the courage to change the things I can,
and the wisdom to know the difference.*

~ Reinhold Niebuhr

Life-long Habits

*Sometimes when you struggle
And go through pain,
You may fall down
And want to quit.
Don't...
Do not ever give up.*

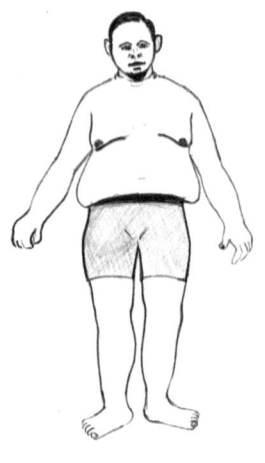
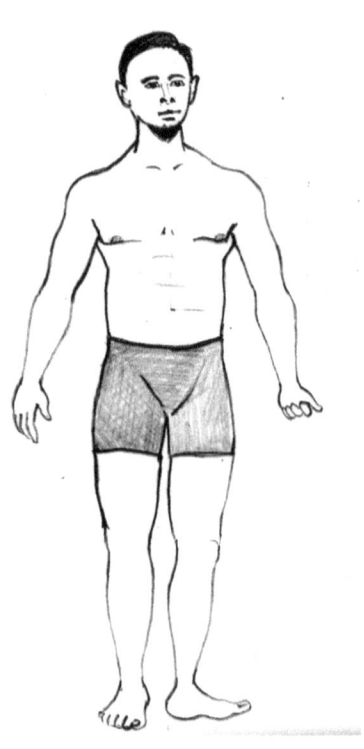

Chapter 15

From "Fatty" to Healthy and Fit
by
Tyler Sandefur

"He's the fat one."

Hands down—growing up as an overweight child had to be one of the most difficult times in my life. Repeatedly being referred to as "the fat one" or described by any of the other negative names I regularly heard growing up, including "Jelly roll;" "Fatty; " "Chubs" is an experience no one should have to go through. I was, however, repeatedly called these insulting names, as well as some others that I could not imagine being called.

At that time, I referred to myself as "husky." Rather than realizing I was actually a medically obese guy at 5' 6"; weighing 194 pounds; walking around with 30%+ body fat, I was in denial about myself and my unhealthy eating habits.

Sometimes, I woke up wondering: *How did I, of all people, become this epitome of adolescent unhealthy living?* When I finally sat down and thought about what made me become obese, I realized it was not just one thing, but a culmination of factors. I watched too much TV. My diet was not only unhealthy, but fattening and lacking the nutrients that I needed. I did not exercise regularly.

On an average school day, I would come home to an empty house to find a fully stocked refrigerator, an inviting couch and an X-Box 360. Every afternoon after school I would drop my backpack right inside my bedroom door. Instead of completing my my homework, I would head straight to the kitchen and make whatever sounded good; typically, not a healthy choice. For example, a favorite snack of mine would include a Dr Pepper, potato chips, and a huge slice of cake that Mom had just baked. I did not care about the flavor of the cake or the kind of foods I ate, just as long as they tasted good to me.

In addition to making poor food choices, I developed another bad habit of disregarding my stomach when it would tell me I was full. No matter how much food I put on my plate, I felt obligated to eat every last bite. In fact, I was not only eating unhealthy when I got home from school, I routinely started every morning the same way.

When I woke up, if my mom was not home before I caught the bus to school, my unhealthy approach to food was a "do whatever I wanna do because I feel like it" mentality. For breakfast I might eat leftover Chinese food or pizza from the night before with a soft drink on the side. If I had any potato chips left over, I might help myself to several more servings.

After breakfast, when I took my shirt off to shower and studied myself in the mirror, I felt disgusted with what I saw. I could not stand the body that the mirror reflected. My image, however, reflected the choices I had been living with for the past few years.

Two years later, I decided to adopt the lifestyle I live today; one that I am proud of. Along with making healthy choices pertaining to food, I began to work out every day after school. When several "friends" told me, "Man, you can't lose weight," I determined that, with God's help, I would do what they said could not be done.

As I continued to eat a more healthy diet and exercise regularly, I not only saw the numbers on the scales begin to drop, I began to slim down. The changes I saw in my body, and the increased energy I experienced, made it easy for me to stay motivated. I realized that the only person who could stop me from getting in shape would be me and me alone.

I adopted boxing as my passion and with the help of my coach, made a complete physical transformation. At first, boxing served as just a way to lose weight. I soon realized, however, that like a number of teenagers, I had a lot of anger and stress that needed to be released. For me, punching something turned out to be the perfect solution.

Every afternoon after training, instead of reaching for a soda, I would reach for water and a piece of fruit or some other healthy alternative to cake and chips. I quickly learned that I needed both aspects of my new lifestyle to stay in shape; exercise and eating right. If I went to the gym, but drowned myself in soda and greasy foods when I got home, it would erase all the hard work I had done.

Each day, I am thankful to have evolved from an unconfident, overweight child to an athletic young man with a newfound sense of motivation and self-worth. Recently, it came to me that I could not make such a change in my own strength. I know that it was only through the strength and wisdom God gave me that made the change possible. As Luke 18:27 reminds me, I know: "...The things which are impossible with men are possible with God." Hands down—living as a healthy, energetic young man has to be one the most rewarding times in my life.

Tyler's Update:

Get back up and start again.

Since sharing my experience as an overweight, unhealthy teen, I have learned that when I fall off the metaphorical horse that I have to get up and start over again.

I have also learned that to maintain my ideal weight, energy, and health, I cannot resort to extreme approaches to dieting, nutrition, and exercising. These tactics, particularly fad diets, do not work in the long run. Instead, adopting a sustainable and convenient lifestyle and eating plan works best for me.

In the past, I did not believe the cliché, "You are what you eat." Now, further down the road in life, I not only believe this fact; this potent saying reminds me that no one can out-train a bad diet. None of us can exercise away poor eating habits. What we eat will catch up with us. Whether we accept or believe it—we are what we eat. In life, the choices we make each day will come back later to manifest themselves.

I encourage parents with children who struggle like me in my past not to make excuses for them. Parents need to help their kids develop healthy eating and exercise choices.

As I strive to continue making healthy choices, I am still learning. I encourage myself and others that some days I may fail to do what I need to do. When that happens, I remember as Matthew 26:41 recounts, "Watch and pray, lest you enter into temptation. The spirit indeed *is* willing, but the flesh *is* weak." When I fail, I pray and trust God to strengthen my flesh and help me to get back up and start again.

shELAH's Note:

Tyler's story reminds me that in the physical as well as in the spiritual realms—we are what we "eat." What we feed our bodies and our minds does matter. Instead of conforming to the provincial "way of the world" in what we "eat," Romans 12:2 directs us to "...be transformed..." by the renewing of our minds, to trust and prove that God's will and ways work best.

Like Tyler, I pray that I continue to learn more of God's will and ways; that I deliberately choose to follow His Son, Jesus Christ. After all, as recorded in John 14:6, Jesus said, "I am the way...."

When we fall, Jesus will help us to get back up and start again.

As God gives each of us
Only one physical body
To care for and live in,
We should take care
To care for
This priceless gift.

Chapter 16

Time to Reduce Salt
by
Freda Gore

"Are you sure?" I asked my doctor when she discussed the results of my yearly exam. "I can't believe I have high blood pressure." I did not understand how this could happen to me as I exercised most days. *Even though I have gained a few extra pounds over the years, I am not over-weight. Besides, people normally gain weight as they age,* I consoled myself.

"Freda, your blood pressure measured 170/98. That's way too high. I am prescribing blood pressure medication for you to start taking today. If you do not get your blood pressure under control—you could have a stroke. Starting right now you have to cut back on salt, fat, and fast foods. You need to eat more vegetables and fruits and most importantly—cut back on your salt intake."

Cut back on salt? No way. I can't do it, I thought. *I have to have my salt. I love salt. How am I going to survive without my salt?*

Driving home, I suddenly remembered that both my parents had suffered from high blood pressure. *I do not feel sick,* I thought. *I never have headaches. I do not have any blurring in my vision. People who have high blood pressure often have headaches. People with high blood pressure are prime candidates for strokes.*

I cringed as I remembered my doctor's warning, "If you do not get your blood pressure under control—you could have a stroke."

My love affair with salt began when I was growing up in the Caribbean island of Antigua in a family of bakers and cooks. I had been a salt lover all my life. Now, as a chef, salt serves as a key ingredient in baking and cooking. But not just any old salt, however, as in Antigua, we personally harvested our salt from the salt pond, a large natural pond which foams once a year around its shore. Within a few months, the sun draws the liquid from the foam, which then becomes large salt crystals.

When the salt crystals formed into large slabs of salt, often with sharp edges that could cut our hands and feet, my family and other locals would harvest it. After gingerly and carefully removing the salt slabs, we would break them into smaller pieces and pile them together on the shore to drain. Later when the piles of pieces dried, we would place our slabs of salt into large sacks to transport home. We used this salt in our cooking and baking.

Along with other kids in my community, I considered salt harvesting as an adventure. We would search to find the best shaped salt crystals and then pop them into our mouths; savoring the salty sweetness like candy.

How does a hardcore salt lover like me cut back on her salt intake? I wondered.

An old English proverb states: "Where there is a will there is a way." To me, this basically means that if a person wants something or wants to do something badly enough, he can find a way to obtain or do what he "wills." My doctor's diagnosis of high blood pressure set me on the quest to become healthier. I not only wanted to do what I could do to protect my heart and live longer, I was also willing to do what I needed to do.

My doctor stressed that my daily salt intake had to be decreased to approximately 1500 mg a day. My first step in strengthening my will to eat less salt required that I modify my pantry. I checked each of my spice labels and noted the salt content. What I found shocked me. Some spices had 350 mg of salt in them. It was as if the manufacturers of some spices set out to kill some of their consumers.

I hated bland food and like most chefs from the Caribbean, I loved well-seasoned foods. Still, I knew I had to replace those super-salty spices with seasonings that would not make the foods I prepared lose flavor. Somehow, the salt had to go—but the flavor had to stay.

I started by making my own seasoning blends; going back to my roots and using more fresh herbs, marinades, and rubs. I marinated my meats overnight to give them enough time to absorb the seasonings. When shopping, I started paying more attention to food labels. I stayed away from convenience and fast foods and made most of my family's meals from scratch.

The medical community contends that diets high in sodium prove to be a major cause of high blood pressure. According to Dr. Stephen Havas of the University of Maryland School of Medicine, also a leading sodium expert, processed foods and restaurant foods contribute almost 80% of sodium to many Americans diets. Havas states: "High blood pressure and pre-hypertension significantly increase the risk of having a heart attack or stroke. Today, roughly 65 million Americans have high blood pressure and another 45 million have pre-hypertension." The American habit of eating too much salt has placed many Americans' lives in jeopardy.

Although I have not completely conquered my salt intake, today my blood pressure is under control. I am working toward maintaining overall healthy eating habits. Hebrews 4:16 reminds us to pray to God for the help that we need: "Let us therefore come boldly to the throne of grace, that we may obtain mercy and find grace to help in time of need." Today, I, as a lifelong salt lover, am not fully free from salt. I may never eat a totally salt-free diet. Nevertheless, with God's grace, I have the will to control my habit of eating too much of this "necessary for our health" mineral.

With God's grace and help, I am sure—I am on my way.

shELAH's Note:

Instead of being "a hardcore salt lover" like Freda, I have to admit to letting my craving for sugar overcome me at times. As a result, I have become borderline diabetic. To reverse this "condition," I know that I have to do what I have to do—make healthier choices in my diet. I have to eat less sugar.

Some sources estimate that Americans consume as much as 30 teaspoons of sugar each day. According to Ben Dreyfuss:

> That is bonkers. Sugar is bad. Big Sugar spent decades and millions of dollars—trying to conceal that fact.
> Added sugar has been linked to a whole slew of health issues from diabetes to cardiovascular disease. Sugar consumption is a health crisis in America.

Although the Bible does not talk about sugar, Proverbs 25:27 warns, "*It is* not good to eat much honey...." Daniel 1 relates the story of Nebuchadnezzar, king of Babylon, testing Daniel and three other youth, Hananiah, Mishael, and Azariah, for 10 days to see the results of refraining from "rich" foods. Instead of the King's usual diet, the youth ate vegetables and drank water during the testing time. At the end of the test, Daniel and his friends proved to be much healthier than those who ate the King's food.

Like Daniel, Hananiah, Mishael, and Azariah, instead of giving into sugar and other cravings that I know may ultimately harm me, I pray to focus more on eating a healthier diet. I also pray to feed more of what Jesus focused on, recorded in John 4:34: "My food is to do the will of Him who sent Me, and to finish His work."

When I focus on God's will for my life, I know that instead of being a "hardcore sugar lover," I will do what the Bible says we are to do; love God and love others. Like Freda, "With God's grace and help, I am sure—I am on my way."

What could be sweeter?

*God assigns angels
To watch over and guard us.
And when our time of death arrives,
He takes those who trust His saving grace
To live with Him forever
In Heaven
Where at last, we
See Him face-to-face.*

Chapter 17

Whatever You Do, Witnesses Watch
by
Bob Fu

No witnesses...

No witnesses can see me or Heidi [my wife] sneaking out of our small sixth floor apartment in Beijing, I thought that hot, humid August midnight almost 20 years ago. I knew that if we were arrested again, we would likely experience an even more horrific fate than our previous one. Being sentenced to prison or living under house arrest in the heart of the capital of the People's Republic of China did not frighten me. On the other hand, concern that the Communist Chinese government could force us to abort our unborn child fortified my resolve to move forward to do whatever I could to protect my family.

"Dear God," I silently prayed, "please help us. Don't let one of the police officers stationed by our building's entrance take a cigarette break and witness Heidi and me making our escape. Please don't let a neighbor wake up and report us to the security guards."

Ultimately that next year, with God's help; through people He used, Heidi and I, with our infant son, successfully escaped to America. In 1997, as I planned to thank those God used to help my family escape China's ongoing religious persecution, I could not locate one particular pertinent person.

Months earlier in China, the unknown woman had told the worker taking her order that Craig, one of our mutual friends, referred her to our reportedly "illegal" printing press. The woman placed an order for a number of Christian books, paid a deposit, and then simply disappeared. When the unidentified woman did not return to retrieve the books she ordered, Heidi and I used the funds for our strategic escape.

As the woman had not left her name or any contact information, we could not locate her. "Will you please find this woman's address and give it to us so we can write a letter to thank her?" I asked Craig.

"I never told a woman about you," Craig said. To date, we still do not know the woman's identity.

Billy Graham referred to angels as "God's secret agents." I wonder if God employed one of His secret angel agents in the form of the unidentified woman to help our family escape from China.

The night Heidi and I stepped out of our Beijing apartment to escape to freedom, I had focused on the fact there could be no witnesses. The Bible reassures us, on the other hand, that our Heavenly Father employs witnesses to watch us continually.

Hebrews 12:1 informs us that even when we may forget or momentarily think we are alone; heavenly witnesses observe whatever we do as well as what we experience: "...since we are surrounded by so great a cloud of witnesses, let us lay aside every weight, and the sin which so easily ensnares *us, and* let us run with endurance the race that is set before us." Sometimes, the Bible also reveals heavenly witnesses intervene on our behalf.

Forces from the dark side, however, likewise observe us, with evil and destructive intents. The book of Job records two accounts when God asked Satan: "Have you considered my servant Job...?" Interesting to note, Satan could only do to Job what God permitted him to do. Even now, Satan cannot implement any secret, caustic plan on God's children; on those "born again" into the family and freedom of faith.

Jesus encouraged His disciples to remember that witnesses watch whatever one does; that ultimately; no "secrets" go without being witnessed and exposed: "For nothing is secret that will not be revealed, nor *anything* hidden that will not be known and come to light" (Luke 8:17).

Those who have trusted Jesus, the Light of the World, do not have to fear. As we confess our secret and obvious sins, He faithfully forgives us. God's perfect love, reflected in 1 John 4:18, reassures: "There is no fear in love; but perfect love casts out fear, because fear involves torment. But he who fears has not been made perfect in love."

In a world often operating out of fear, license-plate cameras track millions of Americans. Edward Snowden, former NSA contractor, warned that in the US, children today "...will never know... [experience] privacy...." Even in the physical realm, we and our children are not only continually being watched but also likely recorded—whether or not we are doing anything wrong.

Nevertheless, we do not have to fear. When we rest in and follow Jesus, we can forfeit fear and escape visible and invisible constraints which squelch us, our spirits, and our spiritual freedom. During our future days, no matter whether in China, the US, or anywhere else in the world, because of Christ, we can fortify our resolve to move forward in love. In turn, wherever He leads as well as in whatever He empowers us to do, Jesus will enlighten, embolden, and encourage us in the family of faith.

No witnesses?

No; not true. We have a cloud of witnesses surrounding us. The exact number included in that "so great a cloud of witnesses" supersedes my understanding.

God remains in control, I have learned, not only of the days we live, but also of the number of witnesses watching us as we live out those days.

shELAH's Note:

Several reminders in Bob's story encourage me, particularly that Satan could only do to Job what God permitted him to do and that even now, Satan cannot implement any secret, caustic plan on God's children. Bob's story also reminds me to pray for those believers in other countries who are persecuted for their faith in Jesus Christ; to pray for those who may even have to face death or lose their children for their belief.

Job 3:25 records Job to say, "For the thing I greatly feared has come upon me, And what I dreaded has happened to me." According to the University of Minnesota, chronic fear can cause physical problems:

> Living under constant threat weakens our immune system and can cause cardiovascular damage, gastrointestinal problems, such as ulcers and irritable bowel syndrome, and decreased fertility.
>
> Fear can impair formation of long-term memories and cause damage to certain parts of the brain, such as the hippocampus. This can make it even more difficult to

regulate fear and can leave a person anxious most of the time. To someone in chronic fear, the world looks scary and their memories confirm that.

Fear may not only negatively impact our thinking and decision making, it can adversely affect our physical and spiritual well-being. With God's help, however, we can overcome fear.

Do not fear—Jesus repeatedly said that. After all, like Bob stresses, as witnesses, those we can see as well as invisible ones, watch us—God remains in control.

God not only listens to our prayers,
He understands and knows
What we need.
When we trust Him,
Our hopes and dreams
Overshadow our fears.
God reassures our hearts
That the days of our lives
Are in His hands.

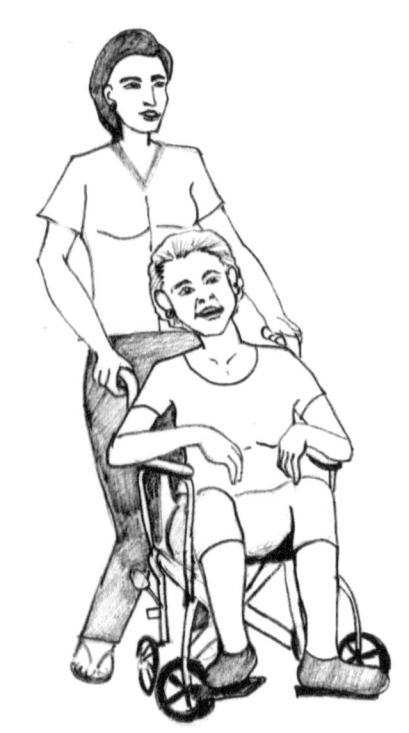

Chapter 18

How to Care for a Terminally-Ill Friend
by
Deedee

"Things don't look good at this point..."

That December day in 2014, shortly after Dr. Mark, my oncologist, had called my family to gather around me, his words shook me and my life as I had been living it. "I'm sorry to report that you have cancer," Dr. Mark said, "and it's bad. You have a rare form of cancer that started in your appendix. At this point, it has metastasized to other areas in your stomach. Unfortunately, we were not able to remove all the cancerous cells."

"How long will I have?" I asked, determined not to break down just yet.

Dr. Mark did not try to shield me from the truth I needed to hear. "More than likely, without treatment, you will only live another year and a half or... maybe two. With chemotherapy and radiation, you may live up to three more years. With the type of cancer you have, at its advanced stage, even with treatment, people rarely live more than three years."

Later, as I lay in my hospital bed, I gave into my tears and the birth of the anger that I have had to work through.

Then and even now, I was not angry at God nor even the fact that I had cancer. The anger I felt came from the unanswered question that churned inside me, *Why?*

Why? I questioned.

Why, after years of going to doctors and going through test after test after test for my constant, profound stomach problems, did I only find out about the cancer after it had progressed to Stage IV?

Why now at the age of 62?

As I recounted the events that had led up to me learning that I had cancer, I realized that it was only by the grace of God that it had been discovered. Months earlier, during a consult to tentatively schedule replacement knee surgery on my right knee, I told Dr. Samuel that at this time, I was not comfortable with following through with his recommendation.

"You know you are my favorite patient," Dr. Samuel teased. "What is the problem, Deedee? You really do need to have the procedure done."

"I'm still experiencing too much pain in my stomach," I said. "I need to settle my stomach before I take care of my knee."

Dr. Samuel initiated the process for me to have a complete medical work-up. In turn, the "old fashioned" exploratory surgery ultimately led to the discovery of my cancer.

Later, when Dr. Mark advised me of my options, I shared them with my family. I also told them of my concerns: "I am not going to take chemo if you're not going to be there for me." Without hesitating, each of my five children reassured me, "Don't worry, Mom— we will be there with and for you."

Today, I encourage others to remember to let those you love know that you love them whether they are healthy or not, even if they, like me, have terminal cancer.

I tell others: "Don't run from someone in their time of sickness or trouble."

When some of my friends learned that I had Stage IV cancer, they stopped calling me and inviting me to do things with them. Some would say, "Deedee, I know you don't feel well...."

"Well," I wanted to say at times, "what do you think I want to do—just lie down on my bed and stare up at the ceiling while I wait to die?"

Some friends and family members have stuck with me. They, and faith in God, have helped me to work through and push through the times when I was not sure I could make it through the side effects of the chemo.

Although I know that doctors do their best to give me and others longevity, I also realize that I am in the hands of a much Higher Power than any in the medical field. I also know that I am still here on this earth because it is not yet my time to die. I am still alive because God has kept me here.

Before that day in December 2014, when Dr. Mark told me, "Things don't look good at this point...," I thought I was in control of things that in reality were not my call.

Today, I realize that my work is not done on this earth. I also know that the days of my life are not in my hands nor the hands of the doctors. My life, as well as the moments that by the grace of God He gives me to live, are just like the moments you are given to live—in His hands.

shELAH's Note:

After Deedee shared her story with me on the phone, I asked her about Lahcen, the friend who had called to tell me that Deedee had a story that needed to be told.

"When in my wheelchair at the airport where Lahcen works," Deedee told me, "I asked a young woman also working there if she would help me. In a less than kind tone, this woman loudly proclaimed, 'I'm not going all the way over there.'

"When Lahcen saw my dilemma," Deedee said, "he helped without me even asking. I could tell he was sincere and felt that even if he had not been employed at the airport, he would have helped me or anyone else who needed him to do so."

Deedee told me that she has progressed from feeling overwhelmed at times to being at peace with God being in control. "I am now able to sing, 'Victory is Mine,'" she said.

Deedee's story reminds me to try to help a friend or loved one, who may be terminally ill, cope with their feelings. We can encourage them to talk about their life. We can ask them to share stories about how things differ from when they were younger; about some of the hard times they survived; about fun and exciting times they experienced.

Sharing memories can help reassure our loved ones that they and their life matter; that we love them will remember them when they die. Recording or videoing our conversations can also honor our loved one and his or her memory.

As Deedee stressed, remember that our loved ones remain the same person as before becoming ill. Most likely, he or she will still be interested in, as well as need and desire the same things. They will not likely want to, as Deedee stressed, she did not want to do—"just lie down on my bed and stare up at the ceiling while I wait to die."

Deedee's feisty, beautiful "not afraid to die" spirit and story reflect the reassurance recorded in 1 Corinthians 15:55. Because of faith in Jesus Christ, we do not have to fear death. We can know, as Paul, proclaimed, "O Death, where *is* your sting? O Hades, where *is* your victory?" Like Deedee, we can be at peace, and know that the number of days of our lives are in God's hands—even when things, from our human perspective, don't look good.

*When we pray
And put our worries in God's Hands,
He takes the worries from
Our troubled minds
And replaces those tumultuous thoughts
With Heavenly Peace
In our hearts.*

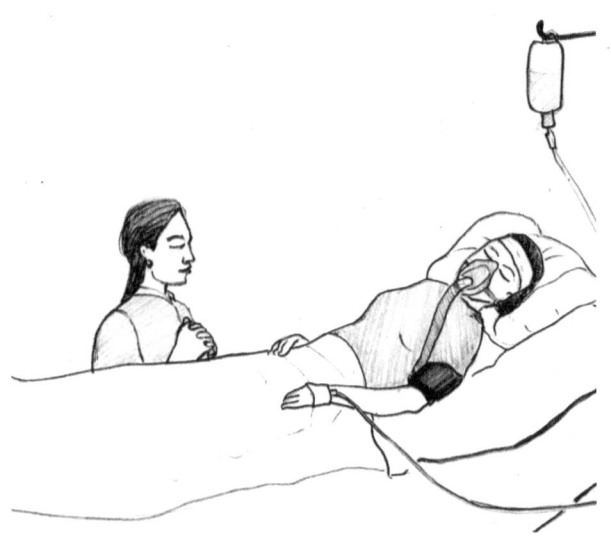

Chapter 19

Prayer: A Source of Aid for Alyssa
by
Misty Aydelott

Alyssa's still here.

The doctors tell us that the fact Alyssa breathes on her own, walks, and talks today, qualifies her as a miracle.

I agree. I know that Alyssa, my 13-year-old daughter, would not be here following her almost fatal injury without God granting us a miracle in answer to the prayers of so many people in the Hickman County, Tennessee community.

On May 15, 2015, the surgeon who met my husband, Jonathan, and me at Vanderbilt Children's Hospital in Nashville, where Alyssa had been life-flighted after a traumatic brain injury. "There is a 99.7% chance that your daughter may not make it," he solemnly said.

"God, please take care of Alyssa, however You see fit," I cried out through my tears.

When friends and I computed the odds that Alyssa would survive to be only .3%, we, along with hundreds of people who cared and believed in prayer, continued to pray.

People I knew, as well as some I had not previously met, came to the hospital from churches all throughout Hickman County.

As I reflect back upon these past four months, I am amazed at how many people have reassured our family that they are praying for us. Not only have people here at home said, "I am praying for Alyssa," many from other states, including Michigan and Montana, as well as from other countries like Switzerland and Scotland have joined us in prayer for Alyssa.

Two words come to my mind regarding those who have and continue to pray for Alyssa… *Thank you….* I also think: *It's not so much the words that people say that I treasure. It's also the way people show they care… in the hugs they give us… by making a point to stand with us when we were in the hospital—especially when Alyssa only had a .3% chance to live.*

At times when I felt overwhelmed, I knew that because of people praying for us, God had given us the strength that we needed. Initially, after Alyssa regained consciousness, she remained hospitalized at Vanderbilt Children's Hospital for approximately a month More often than not, she cried throughout those days. Next, we traveled to Scottish Rite Rehabilitation Center in Atlanta, Georgia, where Alyssa continued her rehabilitation process.

Doctors had warned that Alyssa's personality would likely change dramatically. Instead, we have been grateful to see that the beautiful young teen we know is still the same in many ways. Even though Alyssa's brain injury left her blind and she has trouble sleeping at night because of living in constant darkness, she does not complain. Regarding her blindness, she said, "I wondered what it would feel like to be blind. Now I know." Despite the fact that she regularly experiences pain, each day Alyssa shows that she is determined to become the best she can be. Each week, as she continues her rehabilitation sessions and checkups with doctors, I realize what I hear so often—Alyssa is a miracle of God."

Prayer: A Source of Aid for Alyssa

Alyssa still likes many of the things that she liked before her injury, particularly her favorite food, Enchilada Casserole. She also smiles during the times Ellie, her younger sister, helps her walk or paints her fingernails. When Wyatt, her younger brother, cuddles up next to her, you can see that his presence comforts her.

Before her injury, Alyssa played on the Hickman County Middle School's soccer team. In June, at the start of soccer practice, the team coaches, Matt and Jennifer Brewer, were brainstorming with the team about what they could do to represent Alyssa on the field. They considered putting a patch on each jersey, but this did not conform to league rules.

Looking down at her shoes, Cassie, 13, a close friend of Alyssa, told Matt and Jennifer, "I got it! Let's put a blue shoe string in our right cleat."

Now, before a soccer game, each girl leaves her right, blue shoe lace untied. Shortly before the game starts, the team members kneel down together and simultaneously tie their laces. Often, before a game, after tying their right blue laces, the soccer team members will join hands and yell out: "One… Two… Three—Alyssa!"

Craig, youth pastor of the church Alyssa attends, said that when the youth heard about Alyssa being injured, he often told them, "What happens is in God's hands."

As Alyssa miraculously began to heal, Craig said, youth in her group wanted to know, "What can we do?"

"Support Alyssa's family with your prayers," Craig said. "Pray that God will be with them—no matter what happens. What happens is in God's hands."

I agree with Craig, that God remains in control—no matter what happens.

Doctors can't explain Alyssa's recovery. We have gone from having no hope for her to live; to the point we were about to say our final goodbyes; to thinking she would never be able to walk, hear, or swallow again.

Today, I thank God that instead of Alyssa not being able to function in life, she not only walks and eats, she communicates. Most of all, I'm thankful for answered prayers and that—Alyssa's still here.

shELAH's Note:

Misty said that in addition to the prayers that God answered to strengthen her family throughout Alyssa's trying ordeal, the reminder in 1 Peter 5:7 strengthened her: "casting all your care upon Him [Jesus], for He cares for you."

In his book, *Why Prayer Makes Sense: In the Bible, in History, in Your Life Today*, Ed Strauss stresses that God is not a distant, uncaring deity, but our loving Father. Because of Jesus, we may become His children and have a relationship with Him.

God loves us and wants us to trust Him and communicate with Him. When we pray, we are not to try to impress Heaven or anyone on Earth with our own merits or our eloquence. God wants us to sincerely communicate with Him; trusting Him as our loving Father.

God wants us to talk to Him from our hearts.

Even though God knows what we need, He wants us to acknowledge our need for His help and realize that He alone can help us. When we pray, we acknowledge our human inabilities and limitations, and affirm God's unlimited ability and omniscient power.

When we pray to God as our heavenly Father, we not only verbalize that we believe He is God, we admit our dependence on Him. Craig said that when Alyssa was in ICU, even though Misty and Jonathan experienced feeling overwhelmed at times; not knowing how to pray, their faith in God never wavered. They clung to the reassurance that their faith in His loving care gave them. They trusted that whatever happened ultimately remained in God's hands.

God's answer to the prayers of Misty and Jonathan, conjoined with others throughout their extended community, can be seen in the fact that—Alyssa's still here.

*Seeing the heart of a person
Not only helps us
To know and understand
Them better,
But ourselves as well.*

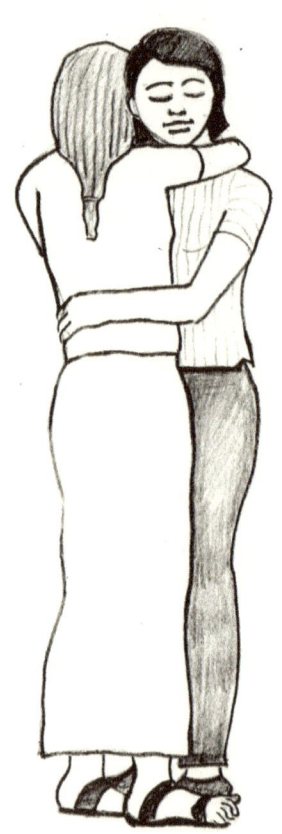

Chapter 20

Hugging is Another Way to See
by
Alyssa Aydelott

No—I do not want you to hug me. I'm not a hugger.

In the past, I sometimes thought that way. Prior to me becoming blind after my traumatic brain injury in 2015, I was not, as one of my friends recently reminded my mom, "a hugger." Now I love hugs. "Why such a dramatic change in Alyssa about hugging?" one of my friends asked my mom one day.

Mom explained: "Before being blind, Alyssa could see a person and determine their mood and personality. Now she 'sees' those traits by the way a person hugs her."

As Mom explained to my friend, the way a person hugs me tells me what kind of person they are. I can "see" whether they are happy and outgoing, cranky and grouchy, or sad and reserved. A happy, outgoing person will give me a warm cuddle as they love on me. Often, I can hear them laugh. A cranky, grouchy person will give me a quick hug and appear anxious to get our hug over with. I can sense a heaviness in a hug of someone having a hard time or a person feeling sad.

I can also "see" things in front of or surrounding me when I swing my white cane from side to side. The white cane, a tool for me and other blind individuals, also serves as a symbol to alert others that an individual is blind and helps ensure the safety of those of us who are blind.

At times, before becoming blind, I, like many teens today, did not appreciate my parents or see the value of the advice that they would give me. Now, I realize that if parents feel that something their teen is doing wrong, their teen should pay attention and listen to what their parents have to say. They are probably feeling that way for a good reason.

Parents do not generally tell their kids what they should not do because they don't want them to have fun. They tell us things they have learned in their lives because they love us. Even though I am blind, I can see things about my parents that I did not recognize in the past; that they do so much for me and my brother, Wyatt, and our sister, Ellie, because they love us. They make sure we have food and clothes. They not only give us what we need, they give us some things that we want.

Parents can often see things about a teen's friends that a teenager may intentionally ignore. Sometimes, friends or those a teen may consider to be a friend, can get them in trouble. Good friends, like my best friend, Riley, and I have become, can advise and help each other work through issues.

"Drama," one major issue that I see confronting teens today, usually erupts as some make fun of others for anything and everything. Kids can find something to bully and taunt other kids about for what they erroneously consider fun. Drama can also come from lies one person may make up about another. I have learned to, and encourage other teens to, ignore lies someone tries to tell them.

I tell other teens, "Don't listen to what someone has to say if it is not true or if it is meant to make fun of others. If someone targets or bullies you and you need help to deal with the problem, go talk to your school guidance counselor. Share your concerns with your parents. Ask your youth leader at church and others who care about you to pray with and for you."

I believe that prayer for someone shows that a person cares about someone enough to want God's help for them. I pray for all my family and friends and those who come to mind. I also thank God for His care and how far He has brought me; how He has helped me cope with being blind.

Today, I encourage teens and even adults who may, like me, be experiencing an unexpected change in their lives—keep fighting. Stay strong. Focus on God and trust Him.

Like Daniel when God brought him safely out of the lion's den and Jonah when God delivered him from the belly of the great fish—in God's time, good times are coming for you.

Sometimes, even though I may think: *No—I do not want you to hug me* when someone I do not know unexpectedly does so without asking—I smile because I love hugs. Being able to see the heart of a person by the way they hug me helps me get to know and understand them better. Hopefully, the way I hug others helps them see that even though I may not be able to focus on how they look physically, I can see their hearts. I thank God that I am now a hugger.

shELAH's Note:

Alyssa's story encourages and challenges me. The way she "sees" a person by their hug reminds me of the words Jesus said, recorded in Luke 6:45: "A good man out of the good treasure of his heart brings forth good; and an evil man out of the evil treasure of his heart brings forth evil. For out of the abundance of the heart his mouth speaks." I believe that a hug also mirrors what a person treasures in his heart.

Years ago, like Alyssa at one time in the past, I did not appreciate the value of a hug. Now I know that hugging in a figurative sense, like spinach, is good for your health. In the book, *The Pocket Therapist: An Emotional Survival Kit,* Therese Johnson Borchard, and Ronald Pies state:

> A research study at the University of North Carolina has found that hugging can dramatically lower blood pressure and raise levels of oxytocin, a good hormone (as opposed to cortisol) that helps a person chill out, relax, breast-feed, and orgasm, although not all at the same time. The women in the study who got more hugs from their husbands had much higher levels of oxytocin and had systolic blood pressure that was 10 mm/Hg lower than women with low oxytocin levels.

One side of a business-size card that my sister gave me also proclaims the values of hugs as it asserts: "It has been said that everyone needs at least 4 hugs a day to survive and 8 or more to thrive." Virginia Satir additionally stresses that we need 12 hugs a day for growth.

Even though I cannot find a biblical directive or any scientific research confirming the necessary number of hugs or validate claims regarding them, the word, embrace (Hebrew: חבק *chabaq*), occurs eight times in eight verses in the KJV. Alyssa's fighting spirit and encouragement to see the heart of a person by their hug, nevertheless, confirms their value.

Alyssa's concept of hugs reminds me to see more than just a person's physical appearance. She also helps me and others she hugs to slow down and "see" some things that too often, we may overlook.

Like Alyssa, I thank God that she is now a hugger.

The words,
"Thank you for being my friend,"
Reflect one of the greatest gifts
You can give someone.
Billy gave me that gift.

Chapter 21

Billy's Story
by
shELAH

"Being different is hell."

Billy told me that after we had been friends for awhile. What hurt him most, he said, was when someone turned away and refused to acknowledge him. Billy also told me that more often than not, when he spoke to a stranger, the person would avert their eyes and look away.

I cringed and tried not to stare the first time I saw Billy that hot summer day years ago while purchasing parts at a water-well supply store in East Texas. *Why in the world is that guy wearing a Halloween mask this time of year?* I wondered.

When I realized Billy was not wearing a mask, instead of doing as usual when seeing someone unique and introducing myself, I froze. Half of Billy's face appeared normal while the right side looked as if it had been melted into a grotesque, monstrous shape. Billy's right eye was swollen shut—the result of being hit with a baseball bat when younger. At the time, although wanting to say something, I could not.

Despite the stranger's appearance, something inside me felt drawn to him. I wanted to meet and befriend this young man. When I asked the clerk working at the counter about the stranger, he refused to relate any information about Billy.

"Why do you want to meet him?" he asked.

"I would like to be his friend," I said.

The clerk agreed to contact Billy and give him my phone number.

When Billy phoned me the next week, we set up a time to meet. From the moment we met, Billy and I adopted each other as friends. We visited regularly until we both moved to different states, and then sporadically kept in touch with phone calls and letters.

I learned that Lymphangioma, the disease that caused Billy's horrific disfiguration, occurs due to rare congenital tumors. Although surgery, the treatment of choice, helps in some instances, in Billy's case, repeated surgeries failed to improve his appearance. Each year, his deformity worsened as the tumors grew back even larger after each surgery.

To avoid contact with people, Billy worked offshore for years on oil rigs. He did not have many friends, but Billy made a point to treasure those individuals who shared the bond of friendship with him. Simple words in one of my favorite letters from Billy reassured me we were meant to be friends. Billy simply wrote: "Thank you for being my friend."

During the years Billy and I were friends, I never heard him complain. Nor did I ever hear him say anything negative about others.

Late one fall, after losing contact with Billy for a while, we agreed to meet again. This time we met in Billy's hospital room. For several

Billy's Story

weeks, Billy had experienced dizzy spells. After falling down one day and appearing disoriented and confused, Billy's brother phoned 911. Emergency personnel transported Billy to the hospital in Monroe, Georgia, where I saw him the day after he had been admitted.

When I visited Billy, he appeared a bit shaky. As I hugged him, I noticed that his disease had disfigured his face even more than I remembered. His nose had dramatically shifted to the left side of his face, yet Billy's spirit was not disfigured.

He no longer worked, he told me. He also said it still hurt when others made a point to look down when he approached them. Other than that, Billy said he was doing fine.

The week after Billy and I visited in his hospital room, he phoned to tell me he had been scheduled for major surgery to remove a brain tumor. Hopefully, Billy said, this would provide relief from the dizzy spells and excruciating headaches he experienced. Billy and I prayed several times over the phone throughout the next few weeks. I planned to be at the hospital during his surgery scheduled in January 2008.

When Jerry, one of my brothers. became seriously ill, I Phoned Billy to tell him I could not be there during his surgery. I planned to visit with him when Jerry became stable. I reassured Billy that I looked forward to seeing him as soon as I could after his surgery.

"I'll be all right," Billy said. "You stay there with your brother."

On the day of the surgery, Billy's brother phoned me with the news: "Billy died during the surgery."

I cried, and in a selfish way, I felt sorry Billy died. I knew that I would miss my friend. In my heart, however, I was glad for Billy. I know that death did not end his life; that Billy is alive with a new face in Heaven.

"If ever anybody deserved to die, it was Billy," Daniel, my youngest son, said when I told him that Billy died during surgery. At first, I did not respond.

Later, when I thought about Daniel's words, I knew them to be true. Billy deserved to die and go to Heaven more than anybody we both knew. Billy, however, was not dead, but alive in Heaven because he had trusted Jesus as his personal Savior.

Billy and I shared two kinds of love. Philia, one of these, according to Greek philosophers, means friendship and portrays one of three ways to define love. In this type of love, a person helps those who help him and loves those who return his love. Agape love, however, the second kind of love Billy and I shared, portrays the love of God which works in the human heart and extends to every human being.

A person extends agape love to others because God loves them. The apostle Paul explained this love in I Corinthians 13:4–8 as he wrote:

> Love suffers long *and* is kind; love does not envy; love does not parade itself, is not puffed up; does not behave rudely, does not seek its own, is not provoked, thinks no evil; does not rejoice in iniquity, but rejoices in the truth; bears all things, believes all things, hopes all things, endures all things. Love never fails.

I believe that friends not only need to share philia but also agape love. Today, many people with physical deformities or challenges feel unappreciated, uncared for, or unloved. So do some of those considered beautiful or handsome people. When we befriend and love people God's way, we see more than their physical attributes. Sometimes, we may need to hold their hands and listen intently to what they have to say. Other times, they may need us to cry or laugh with them. All the time, we need to pray for them—no matter their physical appearance.

Although a horrible, disfiguring disease marred Billy's face, he left a beautiful mark on my world.

One day, when I see him again in Heaven, I know that even though Billy will be wearing his new face, I will recognize him. I plan to give Billy a hug and tell him the same words he once wrote to me. "Thank you for being my friend."

Love never fails.
  ~ *1 Corinthians 13:8a*

Life-long Memories

*Do your best in everything
So that in the end,
You won't end up regretting
Not doing your best.*
           - Unknown

Chapter 22

What Daddy Taught Me
by
Alton Perser

"Son, whether digging ditches for a dollar an hour or running a company for a hundred dollars an hour, always do the job to the best of your ability. That way when you go home at night, you can rest easy, knowing you did the best you could do," my dad often told me before he died.

In my work at Walmart, I sometimes hear people complain about the newly-implemented salary cap policy, "There's no incentive to push yourself," they say. "You're already maxed out on salary." Hearing these attitudes suggesting that a person might not do his best work due to less money aggravates me. Like my dad, who died three and a half years ago, I believe that when a man takes a job, he should always give 110% of his effort. He should make a commitment to do his best, no matter how much he is being paid.

When I was 14, an elderly lady who lived on a fixed income hired me to mow her yard. At the time, although I usually charged much more, she could only pay me $5.00. Another neighbor noticed the care and detail I put into my efforts as I worked in this lady's yard.

"You really are doing too much work for what you are being

paid," he said.

Later, I shared with Daddy what the man had said about me putting in too much work for what I was getting paid. My dad again reminded me what I had already begun to practice, "Son, always do the job to the best of your ability."

I reassured Daddy that I would do my best, no matter what.

For as long as I can remember, I worked and did things with my dad. We set tile together. We hunted deer together. We fished for bass together. I remember that when I was a little boy, Daddy and I talked a lot. When I got into my teen years, however, we drifted apart. In my early twenties, Daddy and I became close again, especially after I broke up with my fiancée. Daddy hurt when he saw how much something hurt me.

We again became as close as when I was growing up.

I remember that as I grew up, going to work with Daddy meant chocolate milk and a Honey Bun for breakfast; a Coke when we took a break, and then McDonald's or Burger King for lunch. Back then, eating at any fast food restaurant was a special treat.

Along with providing treats to eat and drink, Daddy treated me with kindness and patience. Rather than hollering at me when I made a mistake, Daddy would say, "We need to do a little better…," or "Son, we need to try a little harder…."

Daddy not only taught and encouraged me to try harder and do my best, he worked 10 – 12 hours a day, six days a week. No matter how busy he became, however, Daddy made time to do things with my younger brother, Sterling, and me.

As Daddy was a perfectionist, his work was of the highest quality. Because of the effort and quality he invested in his work, Daddy typically had more work than we could do at any given time. Just as he taught me to do, Daddy always did every job he contracted to do to the best of his ability.

At the age of 48, Daddy's right knee "blew out" as cartilage gave way. This led to multiple surgeries including having both of his hips and his right knee replaced. His body never seemed to heal after that and he rarely experienced any relief from his pain. Still, Daddy did whatever he could and seldom complained. Sometimes, when we were alone, he would let me know how he felt about things going on in his life. In turn, I told him what was going on in mine. Daddy and I were that close.

When Daddy died, he not only left me a semblance of his personality, the outgoing kind that attracts people, he also left me with a touch of his sense of humor. Like Daddy, I have the ability to laugh and bring smiles to others.

When someone would complain to him about having to work, Daddy would say: "Hard work never killed anyone."

After he was gone, another of Daddy's sayings encouraged me to move forward in my life. "When you get to the point where you can't do your job to the best of your ability, when you can't do your job right—it's time to go," influenced me to move to Tennessee. Although I still did the best I could at my job in Louisiana, I knew I was reaching a point that it was time for me to go, to move on in my life.

At his funeral, we played Daddy's favorite song, "Amazing Grace."

Today, when I think about Daddy, several of his sayings about work come to mind. I particularly like: "If you do a good job every time, it will lead to people wanting you to come back to do more work, and then referring you to others."

Daddy taught me when to speak up; when to listen. When I think about him, I'm thankful for all the things he taught me. I'm also thankful that I was able to help him get through the last few years of his life. While Daddy lived, he made it plain that he had put his trust in Jesus Christ. He read his Bible regularly. He knew.... I knew.... We knew—Daddy was at peace with God.

Today, as I move forward in my life, I miss having my dad around to talk to. I know, however, he would be happy for me; that I'm pursuing my chemistry career. The only thing I regret is that I did not tell him exactly how much he taught me and the profound impact he had on my life. The older I get, the more I realize just how much like Daddy I really am.

Most people who don't know I'm adopted would never know unless they were told. That's how much alike we really are.

shELAH's Note:

Alton's dad taught him the biblical principal. "Whatever your hand finds to do, do *it* with [all] your might...". I believe as Alton's dad that we are to do the best we can do in whatever job we are blessed to do every day.

Alton died February 11, 2016; the year he would have turned 50. Martha, his mom, said that at one point, shortly after Alton joined their family, she questioned, *I wonder if we can take him back.* Within a few weeks, as she learned how to be a mom, Martha realized that her life could not have been complete without Alton.

After Alton died, Martha wrote:

> I had a plan in my mind that when Alton could plan a visit, even if only for 2 or 3 days, I would show him a spot of God's magnificent creation, the area surrounding where I live in Arkansas.
>
> I also planned to try to get Sterling to visit at the same time so that they could share a half-day with a fishing guide on beautiful White River. But then, as one true to life quote reminds: "Life is what happens when we are busy making plans."
>
> Little did I know that God already had another trip mapped out; that Alton would be going in a different direction. Even though as his mother I did not want to let him go, I had to say, "Farewell, my beloved son, until we meet again."
>
> Alton's death may not have fit into my plans, but I am certain that it perfectly fit the plan of God.

Sterling also adopted by Martha and Charles, said that their dad basically taught him the same life lessons he taught Alton about work. Sterling said:

> Sometimes, when I think about Alton, I am struck with happy memories. At other times, the pain of his loss seems unbearable. It did not take much to satisfy my big brother or to make him happy. He did not sweat the small stuff.
>
> I know that our Dad, Charles Perser, greeted Alton in Heaven because he had accepted Jesus Christ as his Lord and personal Savior. I am grateful to have been able to call him "my big brother."

Death challenges us to remember to
Not only treasure the time
But
To also treasure the time
With those we love;
To tell them,
"I love you."

Chapter 23

What You Should Tell Your Parents
by
Brooke R. Oldenberg

"It's okay, Daddy," I said, fighting back my tears. "I love you and wish you did not have to—but you can go...."

That next day as I sat in my bedroom, for the first time in a long time, I didn't even try to stop myself from biting my already too-short fingernails. For the first time in what seemed like forever since the last time I saw Daddy alive, I let my pent-up tears flow.

As I remembered times when Daddy and I played video games like "Mario Kart." I smiled through my tears. Sometimes, Daddy would get upset when he could not understand how to Drive or turn the controller to make the game respond the way he wanted. When he would get mad at the controller, I would laugh and try to show him how to make the game work.

"Maybe it's not the control, but the one controlling the controller," I would say as I would show Daddy how a particular game worked. Instead of getting angry, he laughed with me. We both thought it hilarious that he couldn't figure out something that I and other teens saw as super simple.

Anytime Daddy and I played video games, I usually won.

On days I had a bad day at school or felt like a loser, Daddy would tell me, "Don't worry about that, Baby Girl. Don't let people get to you.

"When you get older, Baby Girl, say about 45, and decide you want to marry some man, I've got a few words I will share with him," Daddy told me. We would both smile and laugh as Daddy would then remind me of some of the words in the country song by Rodney Atkins, "Cleaning this Gun (Come On In Boy)." The chorus subtly threatens:

> Come on in boy, sit on down
> And tell me 'bout yourself
> So you like my daughter, do you now?
> Yeah we think she's something else
> She's her daddy's girl and her mama's world
> She deserves respect, that's what she'll get, ain't it son?
> Now y'all run along and have some fun
> I'll see you when you get back
> Bet I'll be up all night
> Still cleaning this gun.

"You know I will not wait until I'm 45 to get married," I would laugh and tell Daddy. Before he passed away, I asked him: " When I do get married, will you dance with me at my wedding to the song, "Butterfly Kisses?"

"Of course, Baby Girl," Daddy said.

He knew that I loved the words:

> She'll change her name today
> She'll make a promise and I'll give her away
> Standing in the bride-room just staring at her
> She asked me what I'm thinkin'
> And I said I'm not sure
> I just feel like I'm loosin' my baby girl
> And she leaned over

> Gave me butterfly kisses with her mama there
> Stickin' little white flowers all up in her hair
> Walk me down the aisle Daddy
> It's just about time
> Does my wedding gown look pretty Daddy?
> Daddy don't cry....

Several times, Daddy and I cried together as we listened to this song by Bob Carlisle. Now I cry when I think about how that day when Daddy will walk me down the aisle will never come.

"I'm proud of you, Baby Girl," Daddy often told me. "I love you."

"I love you too, Daddy," I would tell him.

Now, since the last time we told each other, "I love you...," I wished I would have told Daddy more often how much I loved him and how much I loved having him as my dad.

The last time I talked to Daddy on the phone while he was in the hospital, I knew the end of his time on Earth was near.

"I love you, Daddy," I said.

Even though on oxygen, Daddy forced the words I needed to hear: "I love you too, Baby Girl."

"I have to go see Daddy one last time," I had told Mom the day before. "It's just not enough to hear his voice over the phone...."

Mom's dark eyes met mine with a silent reassurance as she picked up her purse and keys. "Let's go, Brookey," she said. Mom knew what I knew that Daddy would not pass until he had seen me. Daddy would not let go of life on Earth until he saw his baby girl one last time.

When Mom and I entered Daddy's hospital room, his eyes fluttered open. He smiled and reached out his hand to hold mine. "I love you, Brookey," he said.

"I love you too, Daddy."

Those were the last words we said to each other.

For the first time in my 17 years, I had no choice but to think about the finality of death. Before Daddy died, even though I knew about death, I did not really think about it that much. I had no idea what to expect regarding all that went along with losing a loved one. Some days, I still think about things I wish I could change. There are so many things that I wanted to do with him.

We all die.... I know that. But, I also know that Daddy, like me and others who know Jesus Christ our Savior, will live forever in Heaven.

I know Daddy now lives in Heaven. Despite knowing all that—I wasn't ready to say goodbye.

I miss Daddy.

Daddy and I didn't have a "perfect" father and daughter relationship, but now that he's gone, I cherish the memories of our moments together. I remind other teens who still have their parents to do what I learned: "Treasure each and every moment you have with your parents. Each time God gives you the opportunity—tell them, 'I love you.'

"You do not know when your or their last day on this Earth will be. You do not know whether or not the time you have to share will be the last time."

shELAH's Note:

In some ways, I hate death. In others, I am thankful for it. I hate the finality of death and that we as humans have no control over its power. Unlike the goodbyes we say to someone we will see again, with this final goodbye, as Brooke learned with her Dad's death, we do not have the opportunity to talk with a person again on this side of Heaven.

I am thankful for the uncertainty that encompasses the time of a person's death. Not knowing when death might come causes me to realize that ultimately God holds even the last breath I will breathe in His hands.

In 1 Corinthians 15:54–58: Paul reminds us that because Jesus Christ conquered death, when we trust Him, we do not have to fear:

> So when this corruptible has put on incorruption, and this mortal has put on immortality, then shall be brought to pass the saying that is written:
>
> Death is swallowed up in victory. O Death, where is your sting? O Hades, where is your victory?
>
> The sting of death is sin, and the strength of sin is the law. But thanks be to God, who gives us the victory through our Lord Jesus Christ.
>
> Therefore, my beloved brethren, be steadfast, immovable, always abounding in the work of the Lord, knowing that your is not in vain in the Lord.

Brooke's story reminds us to treasure the time God gives us to spend with someone. It also encourages us to tell them, "I love you" before the time comes when we no longer have that opportunity.

No matter your age
God can still use you.
You are as old as your doubts and fears—
As young as your hope and faith.

Chapter 24

When Leo Invited Himself Over
by
Dr. John Hall

"Dr. Hall, can you use a broken-down old man like me in Mexico?"

I had to smile. I had no intentions of recruiting a 72-year-old gentleman into the demanding mission life. *No, really I can't,* I thought. *I've got enough patients already, thank you.*

Instead of expressing my negative perception, as I did not want to discourage Leo, I simply said, "Well, I really don't know, Sir. One day, come on down, and if the Lord shows you and He shows me that you are to stay, well then—you can just stay. If you find out that the life of a missionary is not what you thought, you can always move back to the States."

Leo, a "retired" carpenter, and Mae, his wife, moved to the mission right after the earthquake in Cordoba. As he helped rebuild parts of the mission that had been destroyed, Leo spoke only one word of Spanish, "Si." Yet everywhere he went, Leo made people love him.

In Spanish, Leo means, "Lion." Like his namesake, Leo sometimes spoke with a roar. At times Leo became uptight when he did not understand the native Indian language or the boys could not understand his foreign carpentry instructions. Frustrated and red-faced, he would "roar" out at the boys. "Watch it now! You're getting off the mark! I already told you before—don't do it that way!"

When I confronted Leo about his impatience, his gruff voice softened. "Aw, now Doc, you know I don't mean nothing. My hollerin' is just my way. I've been herding mules all my life."

Despite his health problems, Leo taught me a truth about age. A man is just as old as his doubts and fears. He is as young as his hope and faith. As Leo taught the boys plumbing, electrical wiring, basic construction, mechanics and welding, he showed them that the Lord could even use an "old" man like himself. Though 72 when he came to the mission—Leo was young.

At the age of eight, Leo lost his right leg after a horse he had been riding, fell on him. The doctor amputated his limb on the kitchen table in Leo's home. Because of his loss, others repeatedly told him, "But Leo, you can't...".

"Try me," Leo always answered.

When Leo initially asked to join our group on mission trips to the mountains, I tried to dissuade him. "Leo, you can't walk as far as we have to go to reach those villages. You...".

"Try me," Leo said. My concerns eluded Leo. Even at my age, 47, with two healthy legs, the miles exhausted me. Still, Leo thought he could do whatever we did. He not only said so—he proved it.

Sometimes on treks outside the mission, Leo took his chainsaw along to cut down trees. Then he showed the Indians how to chop up logs for outhouses and make boards for building. Leo repaired gasoline motors for grist mills (grist were used for tortillas). He installed electric lights. Then, after work, he took off his artificial leg and swam in the river as if he were one of the boys.

If this "old" man could do all he did—with one wooden leg, some younger Indians reasoned, *why can't we build things too?* Because of Leo's influence, the natives built several churches.

Leo helped put a little order back into a world that the earthquake had badly shaken. From Leo's experience as a farmer, We learned how to raise pigs for profit. He taught us how to install the first sheetrock in our region. When he built classrooms for the mission, he then used the building project to teach classes in construction.

One day I saw Leo packing and loading suitcases into his truck. "Leo, what's going on here? What do you think you're doing?"

"I'm going back home, Doc."

When Leo and Mae left Mexico to move back to Dallas, Texas, I cried.

Three months later, Leo had to be hospitalized with heart problems. His last words to me when I flew to Dallas and visited him were, "Doc, we had us a good time together. I'm happy; you keep on. I'll see you later with Him."

Leo never wanted personal praise. In fact, he specifically told me, "Doc, now don't you go and say much about me at my funeral. I've loved my Lord. Now I just want to go home and see Him. There's only one thing I want the people to know about me—that's my Jesus."

Leo went to his heavenly home in August of 1977. The earthly house he built in Cordoba still stands. So does the simple, uncomplicated testimony this man's life gave. Along with the artificial leg hanging in the workshop at the mission, lives the memory of a simple carpenter who loved his Lord.

Leo often told me, "Ever since the Lord called me to Himself, I wanted to be useful and serve Him. I wanted to do this; then I wanted to do that; then something else. God always told me, "Now

Leo, you just be still. You be ready. When I'm ready—I'll call you."

God called. Leo was ready.

shELAH's Note:

Although I never met Leo, I know that one day in Heaven I will. Leo's life reminds me of the reassurance in 2 Corinthians 5:1: "For we know that if our earthly house, this tent is destroyed, we have a building from God, a house not made with hands, eternal in the heavens." No matter what our age, we would do good to, like Leo, make time as Psalm 46:10 reminds us: "Be still..." and be ready to hear our Heavenly Father's call to serve others in love.

In his article, "What to do in Old Age," Chuck Gallozzi shares 13 tips about aging without growing "old." Three of my favorites include:

1. Keep busy. Regardless of your age, engage in life fully. If you're not active, you're not living.

2. Laugh. Laughter is a valuable aid to our well-being. It keeps us young by boosting our physical and psychological health.

3. Hold onto your faith, hope and dreams. "Nobody grows old by merely living a number of years. People grow old by deserting their ideals. Years may wrinkle the skin, but to give up wrinkles the soul... You are as young as your faith, as old as your doubt; as young as your self-confidence, as old as your fear; as young as your hope, as old as your despair" (Douglas MacArthur, 1880–1964).

Despite Leo at times considering himself to be "a broken-down old man," he kept busy, laughed, and held onto his faith, hope and dreams. I pray to remember to do the same, no matter how I may feel.

I pray to also remember the truth Leo taught Dr. Hall about age, we are only as old as our doubts and fears—we are just as young as our faith and hope.

A grandfather can either leave
Painful memories
Or
A legacy of love
In their grandchild's heart—
For a lifetime.

Chapter 25

Fighter Turned to Prayer
by
Jerry "Gator" Arhelger

"Hey, Mister—you want to fight?"

From the stories my maternal grandfather, Early Whitfield, and several other people, including my grandmother, Lois, told me before Grandpa became a Christian, he loved to fight. Sometimes, he would yell out the challenge to someone simply walking down the road past his house—"You want to fight?"

But then, one day after years of fighting and drinking, Grandpa met Jesus. Grandma said that the day Jesus saved Grandpa, she heard some yelling from the nearby sawmill where Grandpa, then in his late 20s, worked. What she thought was yelling, she later learned, was Grandpa shouting and praising the Lord for saving him.

When Grandpa got home that day, he took the bottle of whiskey he had planned to drink and poured it down the sink. From that day forward, instead of going to the bottle, Grandpa went to the Word (the Bible), to his knees (to pray), and to Jesus.

After Grandpa Early met Jesus, he preached in three Pentecostal churches he started in the Florida Gulf Coast area. Some days, he walked approximately 24 miles from where he preached in

Wewahitchka, Florida, to the home where he and Grandma lived in Port St. Joe, Florida. At times, because he had worn holes in the soles of his shoes, he stuffed cardboard in them to protect his feet as he walked to and from church.

Back then, most country folks in that area, like Grandpa, did not have much money. Sometimes, people in the congregations where Grandpa preached paid him with a chicken or vegetables that they had raised on their farm instead of cash.

Grandpa told me about Billy, a man who lived in a house alongside Highway 71 where Grandpa had to walk by on his way to Port St. Joe. When Billy saw Grandpa walking past his house, he would throw rocks at him. For some reason, Billy never could hit Grandpa. Instead of wanting to fight when a rock would whiz by him, and rather than reacting in anger as he did in his past, Grandpa prayed for Billy and ultimately led him to Christ.

Sometimes, Grandpa stayed on his knees all night, praying. In time, because he regularly knelt down to pray, Grandpa's knees became calloused. When someone asked Grandpa if his knees were calloused because he used to pick cotton, Grandpa would smile and say, "I just love Jesus and I pray."

Grandpa prayed for family members who did not have a personal relationship with Jesus that they would come to know his Lord. He prayed for those who knew Jesus; that they would stay in The Word and grow not only in their relationship with Him, but also grow more in love with Jesus.

Grandpa not only prayed for others, he prayed for and over me. He often laid his hands on me as he prayed, "Dear Father, don't let Jerry fall into the wrong doctrine. Let him find and live out Your will for his life. Help him to be true to Your Word. Let him know and love Your Son, Jesus Christ, in a real, personal relationship." Grandpa also laid hands on my car and prayed for it; that God would keep angels guarding me as I traveled around the country playing my music.

One day in 1972, toward the end of June, I sat with Grandpa on his front porch and talked with him. I felt a chill when he told me, "Jerry, I'm going to die. I'm going home to be with Jesus in three days."

"What are you talking about, Grandpa?" I started to argue. "You are not sick."

"You don't have to be sick to die," Grandpa said.

Three days later, I learned that Grandpa had gone home to be with Jesus. Grandma said that the night before he died, Grandpa kissed her good night and went to sleep as usual. But the next morning, instead of him waking up and telling her, "Good morning," Grandma said—"Grandpa woke up in Heaven with Jesus."

Grandpa encouraged me to pray and stay in the Word. He encouraged me to be real, to be the man God had called me to be; to "stir up" the gift of music that our heavenly Father had given me.

Grandpa taught me to do what I now encourage others to do—to love and know Jesus, not just in a religious way—but in a real, personal way.

Even though Grandpa didn't leave us anything worth much in terms of what the world considers riches, when he went to Heaven to be with Jesus, he did, however, leave us some things that I treasure. I still have the Bible he gave me and the memory of his challenging, encouraging words, "Pray... stay in The Word."

Grandpa also left behind several old pair of pants with the knees gone, worn out from him kneeling in prayer. More than anything, however, I treasure the fact that Grandpa not only left us with the love he had for us—he left us, living out with his love for Jesus.

When I think of Grandpa leaving us with his example of his love for Jesus, the words in a song I wrote, "Beyond the Veil" encourage me. Even though I cannot see Grandpa right now, one day we will see each other again in Heaven.

> Next time you're standing and saying your goodbyes,
> Think about what's happening beyond your human eyes.
> And the joy like no human words can tell,
> And the peace like no human words can tell,
> And the love like no human words can tell,
> For those who know His love beyond the veil.

In living, Grandpa gave us the very best he could. His life, after he poured the whiskey in the bottle down the sink, showed us that instead of challenging others with the attitude, "Hey, Mister—you want to fight?," we are to call them to Jesus by His love.

One day, unless Jesus comes before that time, I pray that my grandchildren will also say, "My grandfather prayed for me."

shELAH's Note:

Jerry told me that one particular verse he read in the Bible right after his grandfather gave it to him, still encourages him today. 2 Timothy 1:7 reminds us: "For God has not given us a spirit of fear, but of power and of love and of a sound mind." At one time in my past, fear overshadowed much of my life. Too often, I expected the worst to happen.

I could have related to the "woe is me" words of Job, recorded in Job 3:25: "For the thing I greatly feared has come upon me, And what I dreaded has happened to me." In time, God changed me from a fearful little girl who would not look anyone in the eye to a woman not afraid to sit in a room, teaching writing classes to six death-row inmates.

In the "perilous times" which the Bible foretells and warns us about, the reminder in 2 Timothy 1:7, reassures us that God does not give us the "spirit of fear." Instead of a fearful spirit, we can have power, love, and a sound mind.

When we do as Jerry's grandfather, Early Whitfield, encouraged others to do, "Pray... stay in The Word," we have peace. No matter what happens—no matter what powers of darkness threaten to overwhelm or fight against us, because of Jesus and His love, we have nothing to fear.

People who say,
"I'm going to kill myself,"
Usually do not want to end their lives.
They have lost hope.
They want to end their pain.
They need help.

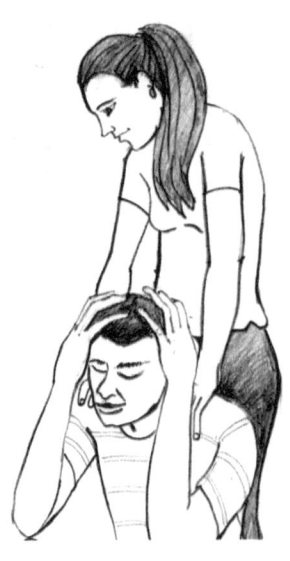

Chapter 26

"I'm Going to Kill Myself"
by
shELAH

"I'm going to kill myself...."

Several times since the age of 16, Troy Wayne Warren had threatened to commit suicide. I married this young man when he was 19. I was just 17 at that time.

None of us who knew Troy believed that he would actually kill himself until after his seemingly senseless death; after, as the following obituary reports, Troy did what he said.

Troy Wayne Warren, a young Keithville [Louisiana] father who suffered a self-inflicted gunshot wound Tuesday in his home, died at 6:20 a.m. Thursday in Schumpert Hospital. He was 20. Caddo Sheriff James M. Goslin said Warren was found wounded severely in the bed of his home around 11:00 a.m. Tuesday by his wife and stepfather. A .22 caliber rifle and several notes, indicating personal problems, were found nearby, the sheriff said.

Survivors are his widow... one son, Randall Troy Warren, one daughter, Dawn Diane Warren, and...

The obituary years ago, published in the newspaper following

Troy's sad, seemingly senseless death, revealed only a brief synopsis of the story.

At that time, I, "his widow," the mother of Randall, 17-months-old, and Dawn, six-months-old, had not yet turned 19. The day that Troy shot himself, Troy's step-dad and uncle had just left Troy when they passed me on the road, driving back to where Troy and I lived. When we pulled over on the side of the road to talk, Troy's step-dad reassured me that Troy appeared calm and in a good mood when they left.

Up until the previous night when I confronted Troy and told him I knew he had a girlfriend and that I intended to follow through with the divorce we had talked about, I had been afraid of Troy. More times than I wanted to remember, he had exploded into a rage that often turned physical. Contrary to what I expected the night before, Troy appeared unusually calm.

When I arrived at the modest country house where Troy and I lived, I started slowly walking toward the back door. I hoped Troy would remain calm while I retrieved a few things I needed for Randall, Dawn and myself while we stayed with my mother.

Each step I took that day seemed robotic. Despite Troy's calm demeanor the night before, I dreaded the possibility of upsetting him. I paused and took several deep breaths before starting to take that first step up to open the back door.

I do not understand what happened next.

Something or someone I could not see—some invisible entity, "an angel?", seemed determined to shield me from going inside the house. I do not know how long I stood at the base of the steps as if frozen in time. I only knew the invisible force would not let me take one more step forward.

When I heard Troy's step-dad call out to me from behind, I sighed with relief. He and Troy's uncle had unexpectedly turned around and followed me back to the house—just in case....

My relief when Troy's uncle rushed past me to go inside, however, abruptly turned to a horrified, sick feeling when he suddenly hollered out: "My God—he's shot himself."

I faintly remember riding in the ambulance with Troy as it raced toward the hospital. I only remember bits and pieces of the minutes and hours which blurred into Thursday. And then, I remember someone gently awakening me as I sat in the chair beside Troy and saying, "He's gone."

Surviving the suicide of a loved one after they have "gone," I learned, hurts. It also takes time. It may also take forgiving not only the one who took his own life—but yourself as well. Thankfully, in time, with God's help, I could forgive Troy and myself.

Why? Why? Why?

I wondered then... and now. *Why do people contemplating suicide not realize they can get help: that they can find answers to problems?*

Why would someone not have noticed what was going on and tried to stop it?

Why would someone reach a point so dark that they feel they can no longer cope with life?

Now, as back then, I realize I do not know all the right answers to: "Why?"

I appreciate the reminder of what one friend said to me when I talked to him about whether or not a person who commits suicide goes to Heaven. "I'm not God," he said, "so I don't know that answer. I do know, however, that a mental illness can be just as real and devastating as a physical one."

One night five years after Troy's suicide, Dawn asked me, "Mom, is my daddy in Heaven?"

"I do not know," I admitted. "I do know, however, that God loves each person and that He gives each of us the opportunity to be at peace with Him. We have to trust God...."

I also know that Jesus waits for those who question "Why?" to come to Him for answers.

Troy and I had never discussed God or death. At one point during our troubled marriage, he had wanted us to start going to church; to try to work out our problems; to start over.

I could not....

At that time, I could only focus on my personal pain. I could not see beyond my own hurts.

Today, many young couples like Troy and I did years ago, struggle with their relationships. Some of them may even contemplate killing themselves or each other. They, like we did in the past, need hope and help.

Troy's obituary reminded me now, even as years ago, that around us someone may feel hopeless and alone. They not only need reminding that our Heavenly Father offers hope, they need someone to reach out to them in love and help them see a glimmer of light in their darkness.

People considering suicide and other hurting people who may be experiencing personal problems not only need love, help, hope, and comforting, they need *The Comforter*.

John 14:16 records Jesus encouraging those who trust Him: "And I will pray [to] the Father, and he shall give you another comforter, that he may abide with you forever."

"I'm Going to Kill Myself"

No matter if we think otherwise when we feel overwhelmed—we are not alone. Those considering killing themselves need that reminder.

Those who hear somebody threatening suicide need to realize what I did not learn until years after Troy died.

When someone says, "I'm going to kill myself," that person is actually saying, "Help me...."

You do not need to worry
Nor do you have to fear
Anything—Not even death
When you know that
God holds your future
Secure in His hands.

Chapter 27

Never Say Goodbye for Fear You'll Die
by
Nathan Wimberly

"I don't ever say, 'Goodbye....' "

Stephanie's response to me telling her and the other workers behind the Church's Chicken counter: "Goodbye" that day, caught me by surprise yet did not shock me.

I understood what she meant: "I don't ever say, 'Goodbye,' because if I say that word, I might not live to see the next day. I'm not ready to die." In my work as a firefighter and as a sheriff's deputy, I often hear that thinly-veiled, underlying fear of death verbalized.

"If it's not in the Holy Bible–don't worry about it," I smiled and called out to Stephanie as I left Church's Chicken that late spring day in 2016.

That conversation prompted me to remember other beliefs that did not align with what the Bible taught. As a "born-again" Christian, I believe that the Bible does not instill a fear of death to those at peace with God. The Bible reassures us that because God sent His Son, Jesus, to die on the cross for our sins and that because He conquered death and lives today—we are not to fear death.

We are not to believe any lies that conflict with the Bible.

Years ago, being new-born in the faith at the age of 17, I wholeheartedly trusted what the Bible said. As a teen, I wanted to hang around with my friends who knew nothing about Christianity or the Bible. I started to let doubt whittle away some of my faith.

"What do you mean you don't want to drink with us? You telling me you quit smoking?" some of my friends taunted me. Most did not understand why "all of a sudden" I refused to drink, smoke, and curse the way I had been doing.

"I'm a Christian now," I explained. "I don't do that stuff anymore."

"Man, it's too hard to be a Christian. You can't do all that stuff the Bible says you have to do. Nobody can…," most of my friends said.

At that time, I did not know what the Bible teaches about God's grace; that Christianity does not aim for us to be perfect, but to trust Jesus for forgiveness. I had not learned that God wants us to love and trust His Holy Spirit to perfect us.

The more I hung around my same group of friends, the less I believed what my great-grandmother, who had raised me in the church, taught me; the less I believed what my preacher preached; the less I believed the truth in my Bible.

Little by little, I started to believe and live the same lies as my friends: *Maybe one beer won't hurt. I'll just smoke one cigarette.*

For the next 15 years, even though I knew better, I continually did what I knew was wrong.

Deep inside of me, I wanted to be a part of something that felt right. In my search to find my place in life, I joined a group camouflaging itself as Christian. When I started reading my Bible as the as the group's leaders encouraged, I discovered a number of blatant discrepancies between the groups' teachings and the Bible. The way this group changed the wording of John 1:1 disturbed me the most.

In the Bible, this verse reads: "In the beginning was the Word, and the Word was with God, and the Word was God." To fit its agenda, the group twisted the meaning of the verse to: "In the beginning was the Word, and the Word was forever lost." To enter this lodge or talk with another member of the group, a person had to say the secret password that the leaders in this group had revealed to them.

As I prayed and invested the time to read my Bible, I realized that I did not want a substitute or man-made "password." I wanted the real thing. As God's Spirit led me to go back and study John 1:1 in the Bible—I saw Jesus, the true Word, in the beginning with God.

Seeing Jesus for Who He is, for Who the Bible reveals Him to be, encourages me to warn others like Stephanie, "Be careful what you choose to believe as well as who you believe. Sometimes, you may feel like you can't change. With God's help, you can…. Remember that you can't base your faith on feelings. Our feelings change every day… every minute… every second…."

Today, when I think about the word, "goodbye," the situation at Church's Chicken often comes to mind. Sometimes, people like Stephanie become fearful of tomorrow.

They may worry, *Am I gonna live to see tomorrow?*

The Bible says that tomorrow's troubles are for tomorrow.

Even though each of us will leave this world one day, we do not have to be afraid to say, "Goodbye."

My great-grandmother taught me that. When she left this earth, I hurt. I miss her, yet I am at peace knowing that she now lives in Heaven. I smile inside when I remember words she used to tell me, "Nathan, always trust God. Keep your faith in Him. Don't believe lies that your friends tell you. Read your Bible. It will never lead you wrong."

If Christ does not return before "my time to die," I will say my final "Goodbye" to others when I complete my time on Earth. At that time, as it is written in the Holy Bible, I will be present with the Lord. Meantime, I encourage my family, friends, and those like Stephanie, "I love you—But...

"But, I know and pray that you also know the man, Jesus. He loves you and me more than we can fathom.

"The Holy Bible tells us all about Him. If what you worry about 'ain't' in 'The Book'—don't worry about it!"

shELAH's Note:

Richard Elliott Friedman and Shawna Dolansky wrote regarding the Bible that one may not be Christian or Jewish or even religious to be aware that the Bible makes a difference:

> It makes a difference partly because of its qualities, partly because of the status it has come to have in Judaism and Christianity, partly because of the status it has come to have in world literature. You can feel any one of a thousand feelings about it, but one thing you should not do is ignore it. One may say, "But there have been times in history (and the present) when people used the Bible for harm: burning 'witches,' attacking 'infidels, [and] defending slavery." True, but that precisely proves that we cannot ignore it.
>
> The fact that it has both inspired people to do great good and been used by people to do great harm means that it is really important for us to pay attention to it—and to get it

right. The Bible is [like] electricity, and it should be handled with care. The stakes are high enough that we cannot afford to be ignorant or sloppy about it. The topics in this book are not theoretical. They are "hot" at the present time because they affect so many of us.

The Bible records that "it is" not only truth, but that it is God's Word. God's Word endures forever. The Bible also records that God loves you and me. Like Nathan, I know and encourage others, If it ain't in *The Book*—don't worry about it!

Even though we may not always
Be in control in this life,
We can be at peace
Knowing that God, in His loving care
Will help us
As we walk beside each other
On the way home.

Chapter 28

Struggling to Give God Control
by
Erin Murphy Anderson

I want to be in control.

When I know I plan to fly somewhere, I become anxious. Sometimes, because I know I will not have any control of the airplane, I not only worry about what might happen, I become visibly upset. *What if?* thoughts often attack my mind.

What if the plane malfunctions and crashes?

What if a terrorist hijacks the plane?

What if someone has planted a bomb on the plane and it explodes and kills all the passengers?

Prior to 1988, traveling by air did not bother me as much as it does now.

Now, I hate to fly.

While attending college in Greensburg, Pennsylvania, at the age of 20, I, along with three other female college students, Kate, Beth, and Elyse, flew to London to attend college for the August to December semester. At the end of this school session, we discussed the idea of staying an extra week to travel and see more of the sites.

It'll be fun, we thought. After all, we had studied hard and who knew when we might have the opportunity to travel overseas again.

Kate, however, hesitated. "I'm sorry," she said, "I cannot afford to stay any longer. I have to go home. You all can stay and have fun. I will see you back in the States."

"No," I insisted. "My finances are a bit tight as well. I will go home with you."

On December 14, 1988, Kate and I said goodbye to Beth and Elyse and left to board our British Airways flight with the promise, "We will see you when you get home."

Typically, at that time in my life, I did not pay much attention to news on TV. The following week after Kate and I had arrived back home, however, I noticed the reporter interviewing our college president.

"Yes," Dr. Boyle said. "We have four girls in London scheduled to come home today."

"At this point," the reporter stated, "we do not know if the four girls attending Seton Hill were on the Pan American flight 103 that exploded mid-air over Lockerbie, Scotland, an hour after takeoff."

Later reports confirmed that a bomb hidden inside an audio cassette player detonated in the cargo area and caused the explosion that killed 259 individuals on the plane. Eleven Lockerbie residents also died from the shower of airplane parts that fell from the sky.

Initially on that day, December 21, 1988, the thought that Beth and Elyse could have been killed in that horrific plane crash seemed ludicrous. As both my friends were usually late, I thought, *Maybe they missed the plane.*

When I learned that both my friends had been on board and had died, I felt as if someone had punched me in my stomach. *Why would God let that happen to my two friends?* I questioned.

When the realization hit home that—*It could have been me*; when I realized how easily I could have been killed by the bomb that caused the plane to explode, I did not know how to respond.

Why was I spared? I wondered.

For several months, Kate and I, as well as many of our friends, grieved over the loss of Beth and Elyse. One day, however, while eating in the university's cafeteria, several of us were finally able to laugh and enjoy the day.

Even though I still missed my friends, being able to laugh after being encased by the heaviness of death left me with a sense of lightness. About that time, however, a mutual friend of Beth and Elyse pointedly stared at me and said, "I'm glad you have something to laugh about."

As a Christian, I knew that death was out of my hands, still—those harsh words stung. Although the intent may not have been to hurt me, those thoughtless words felt like a spear as they pierced my heart. Those hurtful words rekindled the flames of survivor's guilt I thought were subsiding.

When my friend later apologized, we both realized that every person grieves differently. As we spent time reminiscing about the loss of our mutual friends, we gained a better understanding of how each of us really felt.

Years later, while driving somewhere but nowhere in particular, the song, "I'll Be Home for Christmas," came on the radio.

Beth's grandmother had shared with me that Beth had called her mother from the airport to let her know that they weren't late and were there in plenty of time for their flight.

She said that Beth sang the song, "I'll Be Home for Christmas" to her mother on the phone before she boarded the plane that fatal day. She also told her mom to "turn the Christmas lights on. I'll be home for Christmas."

"God, why couldn't you let Beth and Elyse come home for Christmas?" I prayed through my tears. " Why would You do that to their parents?

"Why? Why? Why?"

With the myriad of "Whys?" churning inside me, I continued to cry.

As I cried and questioned God that day, for the first and only time in my life, I sensed God speaking to me. It was if He broadcast His voice through the radio speaker to reassure me: "I did let them come home for Christmas."

Eight words...

Eight words that stopped me in my tracks and yet for the first time in years, I felt completely at peace. That day, I gave God all of the anger I had held about the death of my two friends... all the anger I had held about terrorists... all the anger at myself for not being on that plane and placed it into His hands.

With those eight words, God lifted all the anguish that I had been feeling. *Beth and Elyse are OK,* I realized. Because they had trusted Jesus, they were now in Heaven with God. I, along with Kate, and the rest were the ones who had it hard. We still had to stay here on Earth for a while—missing them.

Sometimes, I may still wonder: *Why was I spared from death during that time?* Nevertheless, I know that, for some reason, God spared me; that it was not my time to die.

God left me here for a reason. While I may not always understand God's plan, I know that part of the reason is to encourage others that in life and even when it comes to death—God, not you nor I remains in control.

Meantime, as we walk beside each other in this life, we are to be there for and help each other "on the way home."

shELAH's Note:

Erin's story sometimes reminds me of David's words, recorded in Psalm 31:14-15a. "But as for me, I trust in You, O Lord, I say, 'You are my God.' My times are in Your hand."

Despite news headlines that remind us that we live in an uncertain, unstable world with so many things out of our hands—we do not have to be anxious or fear. God sent His only begotten Son, Jesus Christ, to secure our relationship with Him. Jesus died on the cross for our sins, was buried, and arose from His tomb. Because He lives today, when we trust in Him, we can have peace that surpasses our human reasoning or understanding.

Like Erin, we can have peace even in a world with threats of terrorism and uncertainty. We can know for certain that our times on this side of Heaven may be out of yOur hands—but always in God's....

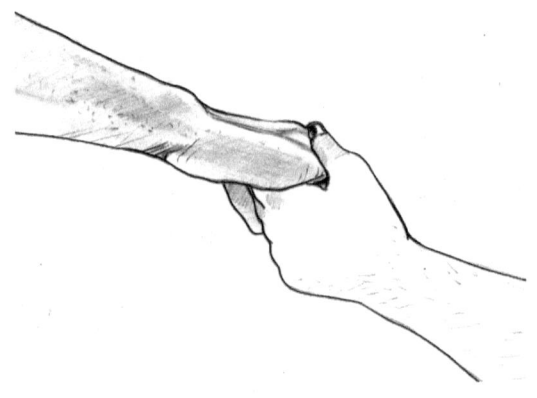

Epilogue

The stories that 26 other individuals share with mine in Out of yOur Hands have reminded me that On This Side of Heaven, a myriad of stories beckons to be shared. As I close the pages of this book, I prayerfully plan to compile and publish a series of books with more real-life stories selected from "Checkpoints," a weekly newspaper column I write—if the Lord wills. I would love to hear your story if you think that it could:

- Inspire another person to trust God;
- Encourage someone not to quit;
- Comfort someone going through grief;
- Motivate others to help someone else;
- Offer hope to someone hurting or discouraged;
- Cause someone to smile or laugh.

Looking forward to sharing more of yOur stories with love,

shELAH

*You can't go back and
Change the beginning
But you can start where you are and
Change the ending.*
~ C. S. Lewis

www.ingramcontent.com/pod-product-compliance
Lightning Source LLC
Chambersburg PA
CBHW031112080526
44587CB00011B/935